BRUGES FLOWER LACE

Frontispiece: *A small corner of Bruges*

BRUGES FLOWER LACE

EDNA SUTTON

Dryad Press Ltd, London

Acknowledgment

My thanks go to Eunice Arnold of Bedford and Toos Driessons of Weert, The Netherlands, for their help with reading the script; to Mary Moseley, of Harrogate for her assistance with the technical drawings; to Anna-Marie Verbeke of Bruges, Belgium for her help with the designs and to my husband, for all his patience and encouragement during our many journeys through Europe so that I might study the techniques and history of Continental laces, and for all his work photographing the lace.

The large Flemish bobbins featured on the front cover were made by Mr Terry Taylor, Ruston, Scarborough. The small Flemish bobbins were made by Capt. John Howell, Halsall, Lancashire.

ISBN 0 8521 9650 4

Typeset by Tek-Art Ltd, Kent and printed in Great Britain by
The Bath Press Ltd, Bath
for the publishers Dryad Press Ltd. 8 Cavendish Square
London W1M 0AJ

Contents

NOTE FOR READERS

The prickings featured in figs 31, 67, 77 and 80 have had to be split into two sections. To work these prickings accurately trace off the two sections and join them together again by aligning the two parts of the reference rule, which appears on the pricking in the form of a thick black line with asterisks at either end.

ABBREVIATIONS

LH	left hand
RH	right hand
RS	right side
WS	wrong side
cl st	cloth stitch
h st	half stitch
d st	double stitch
b st	back stitch

Introduction

My interest in Bruges lace started when, as a collector of butterfly prickings, I noticed a pricking published in the magazine of the International Old Lacers. I wrote to the designer of this pricking, Mevrouw Zus Boelaars of Nijmegen, The Netherlands, who introduced me to the Kantcentrum (lace school) in Bruges. There I saw Bruges lace being made by expert Belgium lacemakers. I attended a number of courses on the techniques and designing of this attractive lace and as a consequence made many friends in The Netherlands and Belgium, several of them being teachers of this lace and always ready with help and tuition.

The stitches used are similar to those used in Torchon lace and some of the techniques may be found in Honiton and Duchesse lace. Bruges Flower lace is a 'piece' lace and not a 'yard' lace. It has proved very popular with those who have worked it.

I have written the book in a planned programme, and it would be advisable to work the designs in the order in which they are presented. This will enable the lacemaker to acquire the techniques progressively, and thus gain a better understanding of the lace. I must stress the need to practise these techniques and perfect the skills.

Many lacemakers in Europe were kind enough to give me traditional patterns which I have worked. Due to copyright laws these cannot be reproduced in this book. I have, therefore, designed the lace myself. Bruges Flower lace is usually worked in 50/2 or 60/2 linen thread. Some of the designs are smaller than they would normally be, so that they can be accommodated. Where necessary, they may be enlarged by the use of graph paper. I have used a variety of threads to suit the individual designs. I hope you will enjoy working the lace as much as I have enjoyed writing the book for you.

1

A glance at Flemish lace

During the last two decades European travel has expanded and the movement of people between countries has opened the door to enhanced awareness of national cultures. Of particular interest to the reader is the craft of lacemaking.

Photo 1a   The right side of a Flemish pricking

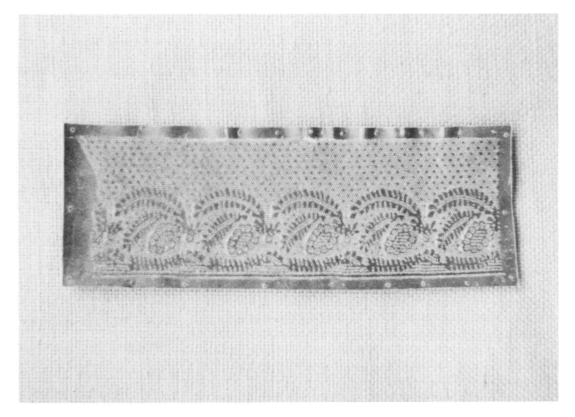

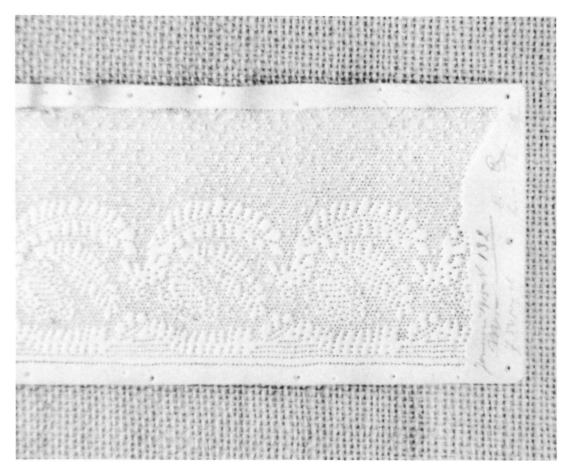

Photo 1b   The wrong side of a Flemish pricking, inscribed with the worker's name, date – 1915 and payment – BF 7.50 per el (a Flemish measurement)

At first the techniques of all Flemish lace were a guarded secret, just as English crafts were protected by the Medieval Guilds. Now, however, the opportunity is there for lacemakers to visit other countries and exchange the knowledge of their laces. During my visits to the Low Countries it was difficult to find old manuscripts relating to the history and development of Bruges Flower lace designs as we know them today.

After the Napoleonic Wars at the beginning of the nineteenth century, many women were left destitute and turned to their lace pillows to make a living. They worked long arduous hours in damp and badly lit surroundings. Originally, fine threads and intricate prickings were used and the designs needed a great deal of time to complete. Eventually the flowers, leaves and scrolls found in the eighteenth-century Brussels lace were enlarged and simplified. A coarse thread was introduced requiring less time to complete the piece of lace.

A 'piece' of lace was in demand for household adornment.

Photo 2a   A Flemish pricking for Lille lace

Photo 2b   A shop window displaying a
selection of Flemish lace

Fashions were changing, and the need for 'yard' lace was in decline. Bruges Flower lace is assembled from leaves, scrolls, and open flowers. These features are joined together with plaits with picots, fillings, leaf plaits and braids.

With some experience in working Torchon lace you will find it easy to learn the techniques of Bruges Flower lace. The interlacing of the coarse threads will soon become obvious. There are a variety of prickings to be purchased, and care should be taken to see that they have the worker lines, etc., clearly marked on them. Today a contour thread is not always used in Flower lace. The prickings are worked in a clockwise direction with the right side of the lace facing downwards on to the pillow.

Photo 3 A modern pattern, line drawing only. There are no pinmarks or worker lines marked on the pattern

A large pillow, 56cm (22in) in diameter is needed, large enough to accommodate the pricking and the bobbins. Flemish bobbins are used to work the lace. They have no spangles so

Photo 4a   Lacemakers in the
Kantcentrum, Bruges

Photo 4b   Three 'sister' laces; Brussels,
Honiton and Duchesse

there is nothing to get entangled in the threads whilst making sewings. The bobbins are always maintained in a fan shape on the pillow, the tops of the bobbins being kept in line. The bobbins are not picked up, but flicked across the other bobbins. This enables the lacemaker to work accurately and quickly. Coarse pins are used, fully pushed down into the pillow to keep the lace in place.

Many lace shops can be found near the Market Place in Bruges, where one will see a variety of Flemish lace — Binche, Duchesse, Vlanderse and Valenciennes. All this lace is made from a fine thread, and is expensive to purchase. In the photograph you will see the inverted shield with a 'B' in the centre. This identification mark is attached to lace made in the vicinity of Bruges.

Photo 5a   A shop window in Bruges displaying several Flemish laces made in the vicinity of the city

Photo 5b   Two Flemish laces: (top),
*Vlanderse lace, (*bottom*) Binche lace*

2

Equipment

Bruges flower lace is worked on a large flat pillow, 56cm(22in) in diameter. This size will accommodate the pricking and the bobbins. The pillow should be covered in a royal-blue cotton circular cover. Elastic or tape may be threaded through the hemmed edge to hold it in place. The cover can be taken off

Photo 6   Two styles of Flemish pillows, used by the lacemakers of Bruges

easily for laundering and replaced again. One dressing cloth is required for the pillow.

When 50/2 to 80/2 linen thread is used, coarse pins are required. If 90/2 linen thread or finer is used, medium pins are required. For finer linen and cotton threads fine pins are required.

TO MAKE A CIRCULAR PILLOW

Materials

59cm(23in) × 59cm(23in) hardboard
59cm(23in) × 59cm(23in) polystyrene, 2.5cm(1in) thick
Three pieces of industrial felt, or layers of velour coating, suitable
    for cutting three circles to the sizes given below
80cm(32in) tailor's canvas, ticking or cambric material ×
    100cm(40in) wide
Strong linen thread
2m(80in) decorative braid

Construction of the pillow

1. Glue the hardboard and the polystyrene squares together with Copydex and leave for 24 hours.

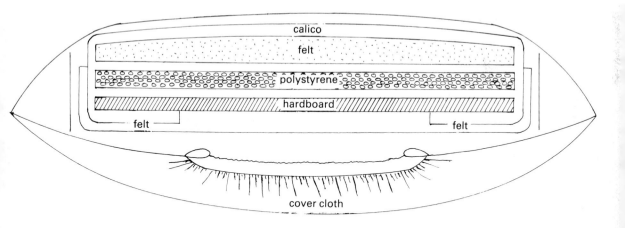

2. Mark out the 56cm(22in) circle in chalk on the hardboard side of the pillow. Cut out the circle with a jigsaw.

Fig. 1   Cross section of a Continental pillow

3. Cut out three circles from the industrial felt; 56cm(22in), 38cm(15in), and 28cm(11in) respectively. Glue the smallest to the centre of the polystyrene, the middle-sized one over the top, and then the largest over them all.

4. Press the tailor's canvas, lay it flat on the table and place the

disk, felt side down, on to the canvas. Cut the canvas into a circle allowing 15cm(6in) to 20cm(8in) to turn over on to the base of the pillow. Using the strong linen thread put in two rows of gathering threads around the edge of the canvas. Tie firmly. Pull up the threads very tightly, covering the edges of the board. Secure the edges of the fabric with a staple-gun to the hardboard. Cut away any thick parts of the canvas, and using a very hot iron, iron the canvas flat on to the underside.

5. The underside of the pillow can be covered with felt. Allow 2.5cm(1in) turnings for the edge to be brought over to cover the side of the pillow and glue in place. Put the decorative braid around the side of the pillow to hide the joins.

DRESSING CLOTHS

When working Bruges Flower lace the pillow is constantly being turned in one direction or another. It is, therefore, advisable to use a circular cotton dressing cloth the same diameter as the pillow. There should be a hole in the centre. Using a teacup, outline a circle in the centre on the wrong side of the fabric. Cut another piece of fabric 20cm × 20cm (8in × 8in). Neaten the

Photo 7   An English pillow on which you will see; a dressing cloth, Flemish bobbins, Belgian bobbin-winder, linen thread, a pricker, a crochet hook, lace scissors and a needle with thread

raw edges with a narrow hem. Tack the right sides together. Machine twice around the marked circle. Cut out the unwanted material leaving 0.5cm (³⁄₁₆in) of turnings. Snip to the machining in places. Turn to the right side and press.

The dressing cloth helps to protect the threads from the pin heads. Whenever the pillow is not in use cover it with another cloth.

THREADS

The threads to be used for each pricking will be specified. The lace has been designed to suit the threads which are available at the moment. Care should be taken to obtain a linen thread of good quality, smooth texture, and a colour to match the linen fabric on which it will be mounted. A good quality Belgian thread is ideal, as it is strong, white, and will withstand hard wear and launder well. Old thread should not be used, as it will not resist the constant rolling movement of the bobbins which will cause fraying and the threads may break easily. It has been the custom to work a sample piece of lace, launder it, and see what shrinkage has taken place. With modern threads this is no longer necessary.

Photo 8   A selection of bobbins from Sweden, Denmark, Germany, Holland, Belgium, France, Spain, Portugal and Malta

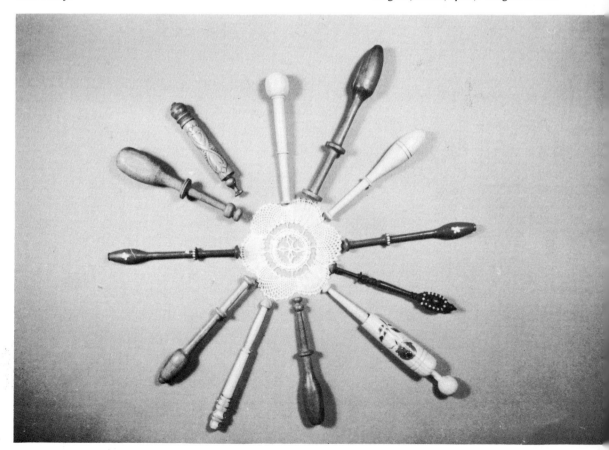

It is better to wind the thread on to the bobbins with a bobbin winder. The thread will be wound evenly along the bobbin shank. Finally, secure the thread with a loop about the shank. This loop has a dual purpose:

a. it will control the movement of the thread.

b. it will prevent the bobbin from unwinding.

Preferably fill several bobbins with thread and then wind a small length of thread on to the empty bobbins so as to make a pair of bobbins. Experience will soon show what length is required. Keep the thread wrapped in acid-free blue paper.

BOBBINS

You will see the general design of a Flemish bobbin from the photograph. There are many sewings used in Bruges Flower lace which necessitate the passing of a bobbin through loops. Spangles would cause trouble in passing the bobbin through the

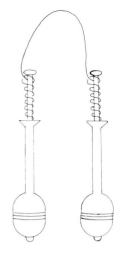

Fig. 2   A pair of wound bobbins

Photo 9   A pin-lifter, crochet hook, lace scissors (with lip), pricker and needle with thread

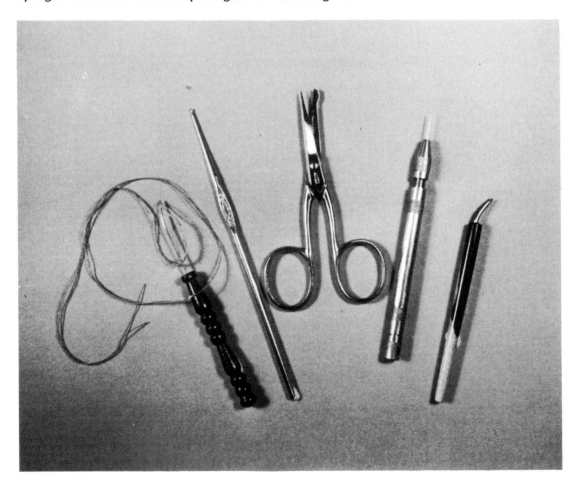

loop. Keep the threads the same length, about 12cm(4in) of thread between the top of the bobbin and the pin. This will keep the tension even.

PINS

A brass pin should be used, size 26.75mm(1in). A pin of this type will hold the tension of the linen threads, withstand bending and remain clean and rustless. When not in use the pins should be pushed into a pin cushion filled with emery powder. When making the lace, insert the pins so that they are leaning slightly backwards and outwards.

CROCHET HOOK AND SCISSORS

A fine crochet hook 0.60 will be needed to make the sewings. A needle threaded with cotton may also be used to make a sewing. The eye of a needle is finer than a crochet hook. There are times when a crochet hook cannot be used because the bar or loop is small. Therefore, use the needle and thread to make the sewing.

The threaded needle is passed through the pinloop and the bobbin is put between the needle and the cotton. Carefully pull the threaded needle back through the pinloop. The linen thread will now slide through the pinloop too. Remove the needle and cotton from the linen loop and slide the second linen thread through the loop in the direction it will be working. Tighten the loop and the sewing is complete.

A sharp pair of scissors, with a lip on one blade, will be required to cut the threads close to the lace.

3

Basic techniques

The stitches used in the lace are the same as those found in Torchon, for example cloth stitch and half stitch. A new technique and special feature of this lace, double stitch, will be introduced.

CLOTH STITCH (cl st)

1. Cross 2 over 3, L over R.
2. Twist 2 over 1, and 4 over 3, R over L.
3. Cross 2 over 3, L over R.

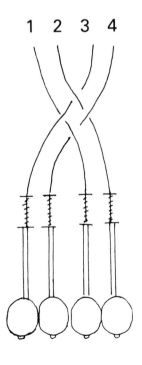

Fig. 3   Cloth stitch (cl st)

1   2   3   4

HALF STITCH (h st)

1. Cross 2 over 3, L over R.
2. Twist 2 over 1, and 4 over 3, R over L.

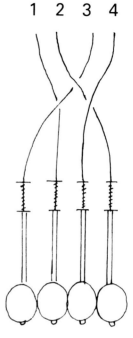

Fig. 4   Half stitch (h st)

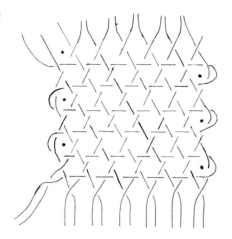

DOUBLE STITCH (d st)

1. Cross 2 over 3, L over R.
2. Twist 2 over 1, and 4 over 3, R over L.
3. Cross 2 over 3, L over R.
4. Twist 2 over 1 and 4 over 3, R over L.

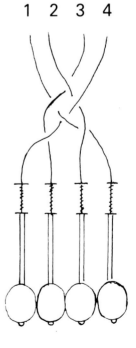

Fig. 5   Double stitch (d st)

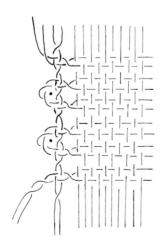

DIEPPE GROUND

1. Two twists on each pair.
2. H st, put up a pin.
3. Close the pin with h st and one extra twist on each pair.

Photo 10   Filling no. 1, Dieppe ground

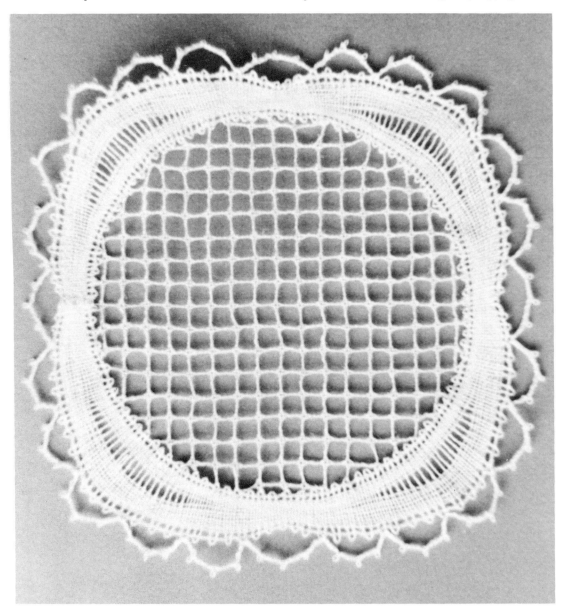

Replacing a thread

When a new thread is required, introduce it by first fastening it to

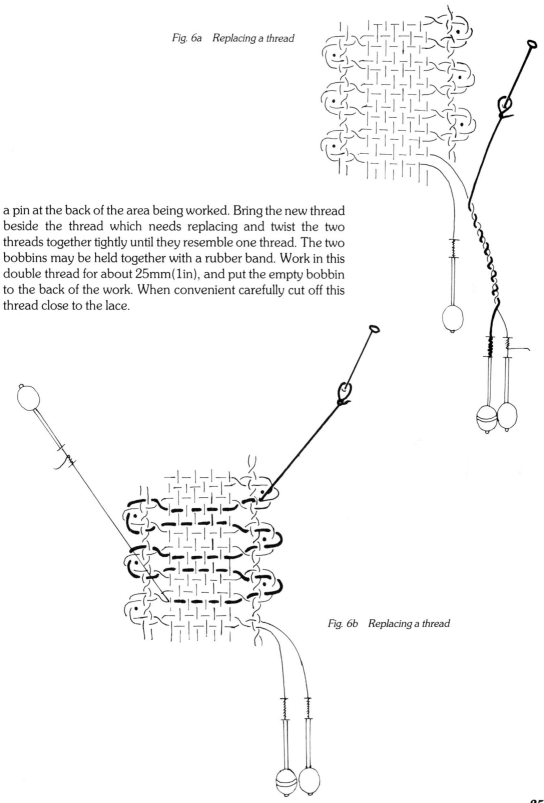

Fig. 6a   Replacing a thread

a pin at the back of the area being worked. Bring the new thread beside the thread which needs replacing and twist the two threads together tightly until they resemble one thread. The two bobbins may be held together with a rubber band. Work in this double thread for about 25mm(1in), and put the empty bobbin to the back of the work. When convenient carefully cut off this thread close to the lace.

Fig. 6b   Replacing a thread

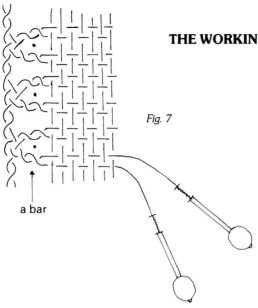

THE WORKING OF A 'FOUR-ABOUT-THE-PIN' EDGE

Fig. 7

a bar

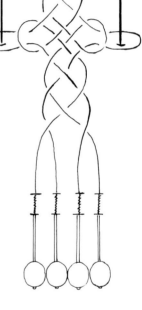

Fig. 8   Working a plait

WORKING A PLAIT (Fig. 8)

A plait should be worked with the bobbins flat on the pillow. Keep each pair to the extreme right or left. Tighten the plait after each stitch. There should be the same number of stitches in each plait whenever possible. The plait is worked with a series of h st.

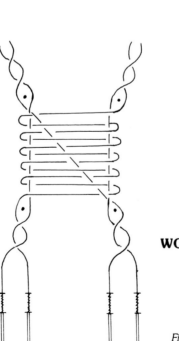

WORKING A TALLY

Fig. 9

WORKING A LEAF PLAIT

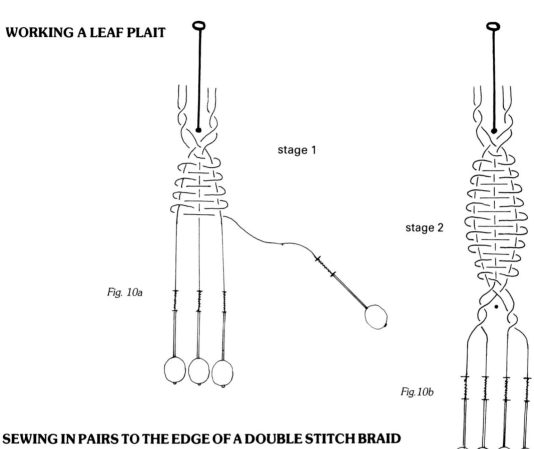

stage 1

stage 2

Fig. 10a

Fig. 10b

SEWING IN PAIRS TO THE EDGE OF A DOUBLE STITCH BRAID

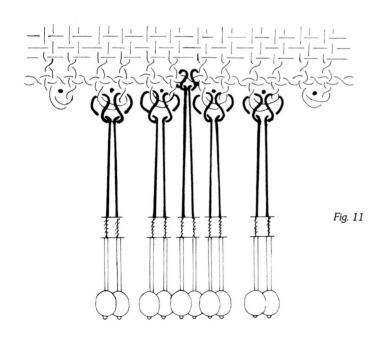

Fig. 11

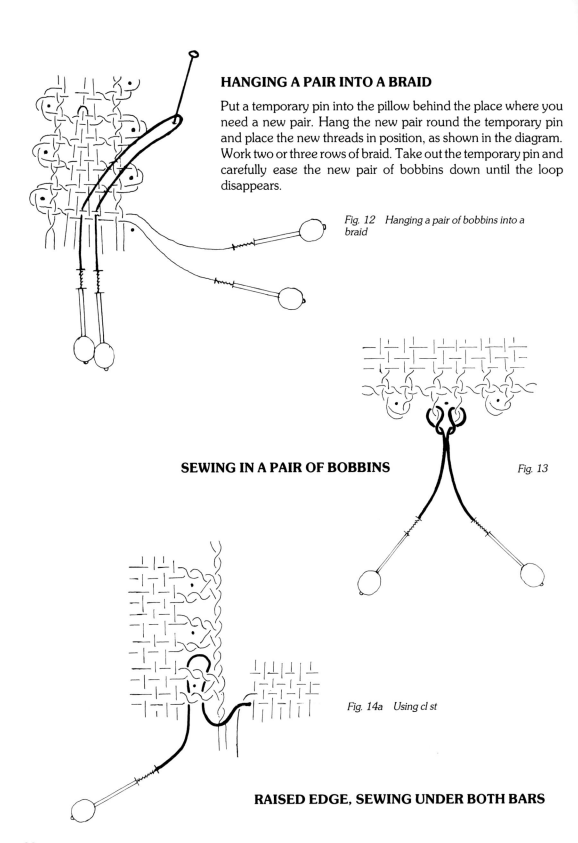

HANGING A PAIR INTO A BRAID

Put a temporary pin into the pillow behind the place where you need a new pair. Hang the new pair round the temporary pin and place the new threads in position, as shown in the diagram. Work two or three rows of braid. Take out the temporary pin and carefully ease the new pair of bobbins down until the loop disappears.

Fig. 12   Hanging a pair of bobbins into a braid

SEWING IN A PAIR OF BOBBINS

Fig. 13

Fig. 14a   Using cl st

RAISED EDGE, SEWING UNDER BOTH BARS

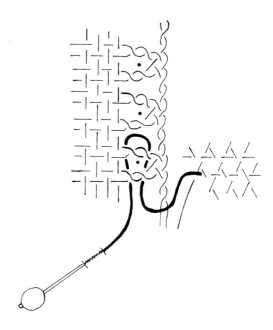

Fig. 14b   Using h st

RAISED EDGE, SEWING UNDER ONE BAR

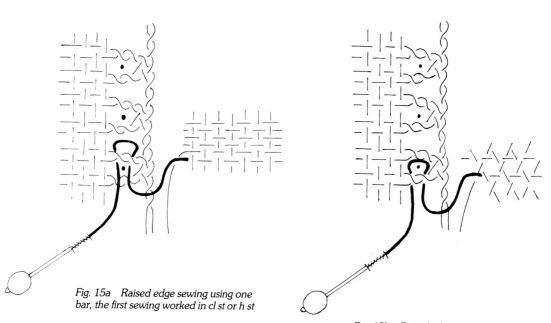

Fig. 15a   Raised edge sewing using one bar, the first sewing worked in cl st or h st

Fig. 15b   Raised edge sewing using one bar, the second sewing worked in cl st or h st

WORKING A PLAIT WITH A LH PICOT

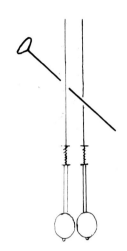

stage 1

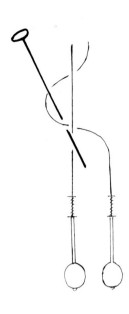

stage 2

stage 3

Fig. 16a

stage 5

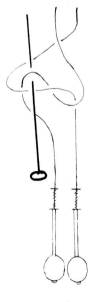

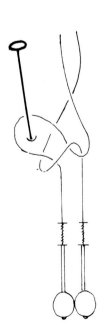

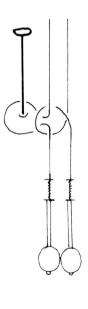

stage 4

WORKING A PLAIT WITH A RH PICOT

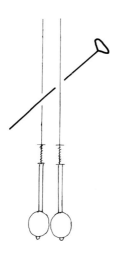

stage 1

stage 2

Fig. 16b

stage 3

stage 5

stage 4

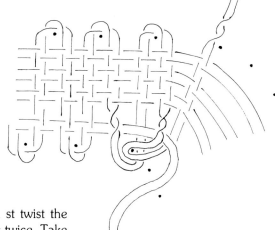

Fig. 17   Working a back stitch

BACK STITCH (b st)

Work through all the passive threads. If using h st twist the
workers once more. If using cl st twist the workers twice. Take
the workers behind the pin of the previous row, under the edge
pair, and continue to work the row.

A FALSE PLAIT

stage 1

stage 2

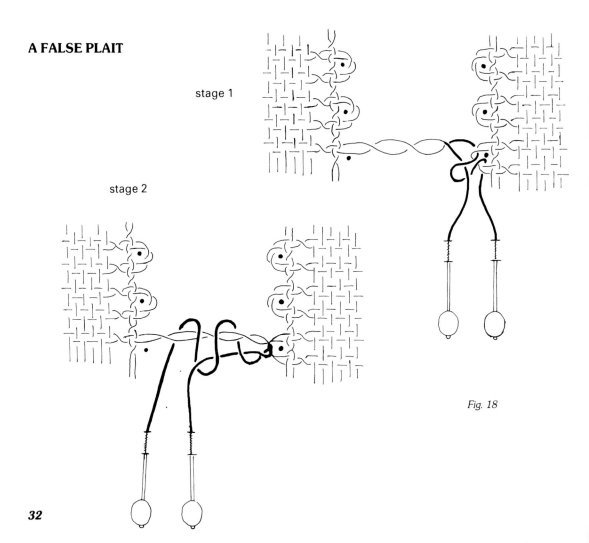

Fig. 18

32

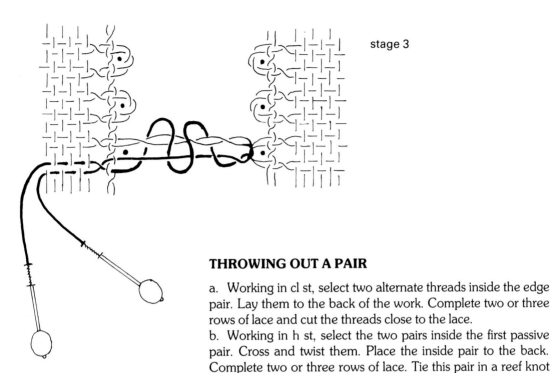

THROWING OUT A PAIR

a. Working in cl st, select two alternate threads inside the edge pair. Lay them to the back of the work. Complete two or three rows of lace and cut the threads close to the lace.

b. Working in h st, select the two pairs inside the first passive pair. Cross and twist them. Place the inside pair to the back. Complete two or three rows of lace. Tie this pair in a reef knot and cut off the threads close to the lace.

CROSSING THE BRAIDS

When two braids are crossed over, they must be secured firmly at each of the four corners. This should be done accurately and neatly. Any weakness in this technique will cause the lace to

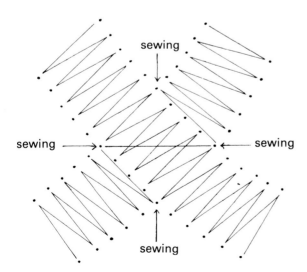

sewing

sewing

sewing

sewing

Fig. 19   Crossing two braids

become unsightly and the braid will be liable to move during laundering. The finished crossing must be flat, tidy and secure. When worked correctly the workers will leave a 'z' shape on the wrong side of the work.

1. Work the braid until the last pin has been put up on the right-hand (RH) side.

2. Cl st across the passive threads and sew the workers into the pinloop.

3. Cl st across the passives and sew the workers into the pinloop at the RH edge.

4. Cl st diagonally across and sew the workers into the pinloop at the bottom left-hand (LH) edge.

5. Cl st across the passive threads and make the last sewing into the pinloop at the bottom RH edge. Continue to work the braid.

PLAIT-WITH-PICOT (see Fig. 8)

A WINDMILL JOIN

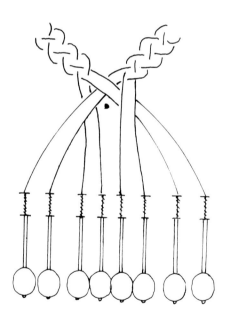

Fig. 20

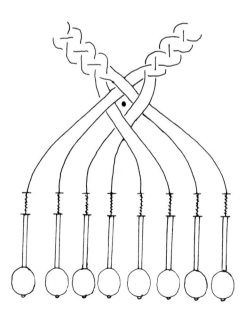

DIVIDING FOR A BRAID

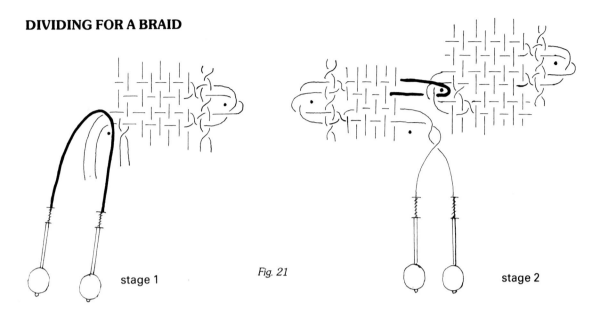

stage 1

Fig. 21

stage 2

TYING OFF SEVERAL THREADS

Start tying the threads from the LH edge. Keeping the LH bobbin higher than the other one tie the first pair once. *Put down the RH bobbin and pick up the next one. Keeping the LH

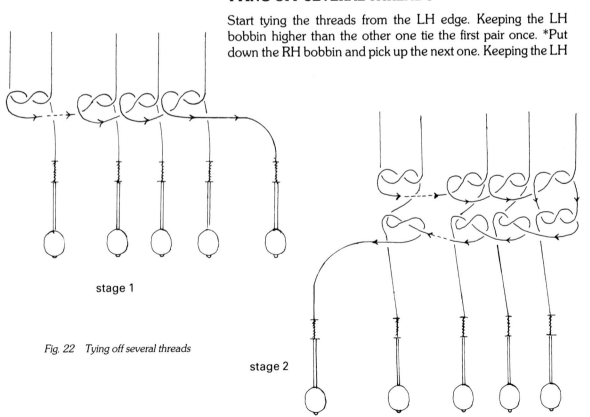

stage 1

Fig. 22 Tying off several threads

stage 2

bobbin higher than the other one tie the pair once**. Repeat this along all the threads and tie the last pair into a reef knot. Keep this pair in your hand and repeat the tying by putting down the LH bobbin (now working right to left) and picking up the next one. When all the threads have been tied a second time take a crochet hook and hold it parallel against the tied edge. Push the shank of the crochet hook against the knotted edge and pull the threads down to tighten the knots. See if some of the pairs can be used for fillings in the lace. If not, cut off the threads close to the knots.

PREPARING THE PRICKING

1. Put the pattern on top of a piece of strong firm card. Using a pricker holding a No.9 crewel needle prick out the pattern. Do not miss any holes. Remove the paper pattern.
2. With a fine-pointed black felt-tipped pen, copy the worker lines, b st, and false plaits from the paper pattern to the card.
3. Mark the type and thickness of yarn required on the pricking.

4

Braids and edgings

Seven braids have been selected for working. Cl st, h st and d st are used in their construction. The braids act as a framework for the lace and make the Flowers, scrolls and floral shapes. These shapes are joined to each other by filling stitches. The cl st braid will be worked first.

CLOTH STITCH BRAID

Techniques used in working the braid – cl st

Photo 11   Cloth stitch braid, braid no. 1

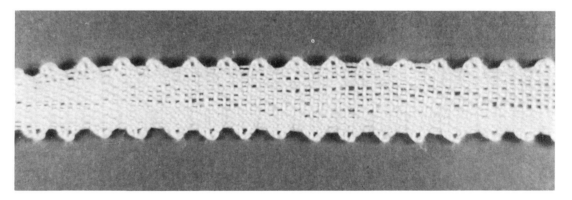

Method of working the braid

1. Prepare the pricking as previously explained.
2. At *a* put up four pins as shown in the diagram. Hang two pairs of bobbins on to each pin.
3. Using the first pair at the LH side, cl st through all the pairs. Twist the workers twice and put up a pin at *b* under the worker pair. Firm the passive threads carefully.

4. Return towards *c* in cl st twist the workers twice and put up the pin at *c*, under the worker pair.

5. Continue to work the braid in this way. Firm and shape the braid, easing the passive threads in a downward direction.

HALF STITCH BRAID (see Fig. 23 for pricking)

Techniques used in working the braid – h st and d st

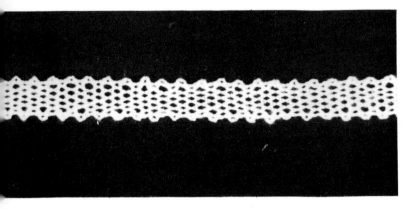

Photo 12   Half stitch braid, braid no.2

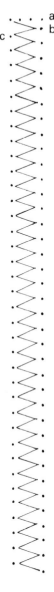

Method of working the braid

1. Prepare the pricking as previously explained.

2. At *a* put up four pins, as shown in the diagram. Hang two pairs on to the first, third and fourth pins, and one pair on to the second pin. Twist each pair once, by moving the RH thread over the LH thread.

3. Using the first pair on the LH side, work in h st through five pairs. Using the sixth pair, work a d st and an extra twist on the worker pair. At *b* put up a pin under the worker pair and close the pin with a d st.

4. Return through four pairs in h st and work a d st and an extra twist on the worker pair. Put up a pin under the worker pair at *c* and close the pin with a d st.

5. Complete the braid in this way, firming and shaping the braid whenever necessary, especially around a curved edge.

Fig. 23   Pricking for the cloth stitch, half stitch and double stitch edge braids

DOUBLE STITCH EDGE BRAID (see Fig. 23 for pricking)

Techniques used in working the braid – cl st, d st and d st edge.

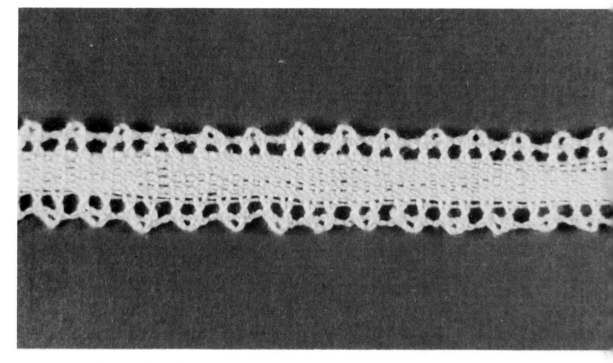

Method of working the braid

1. Prepare the pricking as already explained.
2. At *a* put up four pins, hang two pairs on to each pin and an extra pair on to the second pin.
3. Starting at the LH edge work a d st and cl st through six pairs of bobbins. Twist the workers.
4. At *b* work a d st and make an extra twist on the worker pair. Under the worker pair put up a pin at *b*. Close the pin with a d st. Firm the passive threads.
5. Return in cl st to *c*, and twist the workers. With the last pair work a d st and make an extra twist on the workers. Put up a pin under the worker pair at *c* and close the pin with a d st. This is now termed as a d st edge. Firm all the passive threads when working round a curved edge. The outer passive threads must follow the line of the curve. They will leave an unsightly space if pulled too tight.

Photo 13   Double stitch edge braid, braid no.3

STITCH AND TWIST BRAID

Techniques used in working the braid – d st (*page 25*).

Method of working the braid

1. Prepare the pricking as already explained.
2. At *a* put up seven pins and hang one pair of bobbins on to each pin. Hang an extra pair on to the last pin.

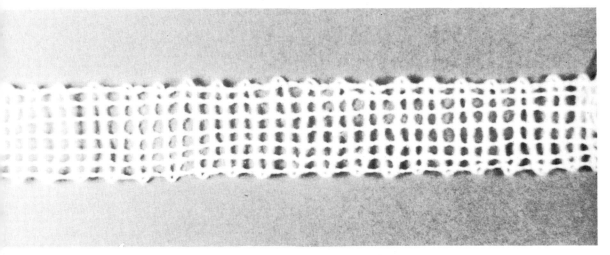

Photo 14   Stitch and twist braid, braid no.4

Fig. 24   Pricking for a stitch and twist braid

```
    1 2 3 4 5 6 7
  b · · · · · · · a
       ·< > ·· c
     ·< >·
   ·< >·
     ·< >·
   ·< >·
     ·< >·
   ·< >·
     ·< >·
   ·< >·
     ·< >·
   ·< >·
     ·< >·
   ·< >·
     ·< >·
   ·< >·
     ·< >·
   ·< >·
```

3. Work the first row in cl st, put a twist on both the passive and the worker pairs. No pin. Work the same with the next pair, and so on across the row.

4. When all the passive pairs have been worked through in this manner, twist the worker pair twice more and support the threads on a pin at *b*. Close the pin with a d st.

5. Using the same stitch, cl st and a twist, work back across the row to *c*. Again, twist the workers twice more and support them on a pin at *c*. Close the pin with a d st.

6. This sequence completes the braid.

DECORATIVE BRAID

Techniques used in working the braid – cl st (*page 22*) and d st edge (*page 25*).

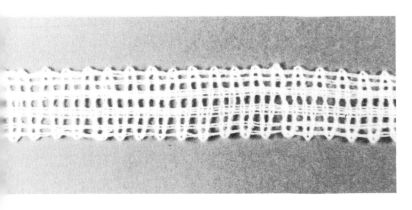

Photo 15a   A decorative braid, braid no.5

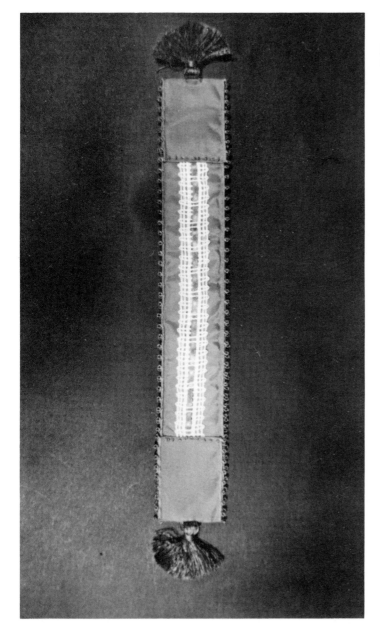

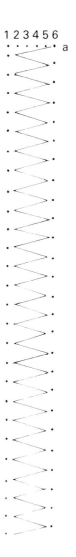

Photo 15b   The braid slotted with narrow ribbon for a bookmark

1 2 3 4 5 6

a

Fig. 25   Pricking for a decorative braid

Method of working the braid

1. Prepare the pricking as previously explained.

2. Along the line at *a* put up six pins and hang on one, one, two, two, one and two pairs of bobbins respectively. Work a d st at *a*, cl st through one pair, twist the worker pair once. Cl st through two pairs. Twist the workers once, cl st through two pairs and twist the workers once again. Cl st through one pair and twist the workers once. Work a d st edge.

3. This row when repeated will make the braid.

41

Photo 16 Braid-with-footing, braid no.6   Fig. 26 Pricking for the braid-with-footing

BRAID-WITH-FOOTING

Techniques used in working the braid – cl st, four-about-the-pin edge, d st edge and b st.

This braid is simple to work when the other braids have been perfected and practised. The braid may be used to decorate lampshades, boxes, cotton-wool containers or tissue boxes.

Method of working the braid

1. Prepare the pricking as previously explained.

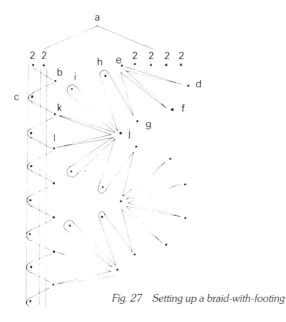

Fig. 27 Setting up a braid-with-footing

2. Along the line marked *a* put up six pins. Hang on the bobbins as shown in the diagram.

3. At the footing edge work a four-about-the-pin edge. Cl st through two pairs of bobbins. Twist the worker pair twice and put up a pin under the worker pair at *b*.

4. Work back to the footing edge, work the four-about-the-pin edge at *c*.

5. Work through the two passive threads to the right in cl st. Firm the passive threads and leave them.

6. Return to the eight unworked pairs. Take the extreme LH pair, cl st through six pairs of bobbins. At *d* work a d st edge, and cl st back to *e*. Firm all the passive threads and shape them, keeping them in line with the outer curve. At *e* work a b st.

7. Work back to *f* and work the d st edge.

8. Cl st back to *e*, work a b st and cl st to *g*, where the d st edge is worked. Firm and shape the passive threads.

9. At *h* and *i*, twist the workers twice and put up a pin under the worker pair. Cl st to *j* where the b st are worked to pivot round the pin and shape the curve. Remember to make the sewing with the pair used for a b st, to hold the b st together.

10. At *k* and *l* the braid is joined to the footing by twisting each pair twice, cl st, put up a pin. Close the pin with a cl st and twist each pair twice. Complete the braid, noticing where the b st are worked and where the braid joins the footing. Take care not to pull the threads too tight.

PLAIT-WITH-PICOT EDGINGS

A plait-with-picot edge is the last technique worked on a piece of Bruges Flower lace. The edging is worked with either two or four pairs of bobbins, and the plait is attached to the braid with a sewing. The technique is used around a curved or straight edge and not where projections, points and openings occur. Work the edgings as much as possible at the same session. Stopping and starting may result in the same appearance as when knitting has been taken up again after a few days. The tension will be different. When a picot is worked at each side of the plait, work the LH one first and then the RH one. Work a cl st to firm the picots and then continue to work the plait. For perfection it is better to count the number of stitches in each section of the plait. This helps to keep an even length of each plait-with-picot.

When joining the plait to the lace the pair nearest to the lace is sewn in first and the other pair is passed through the loop in the direction you are working.

Make sure that the bobbins are fully wound as it is difficult to make a neat join in a plait.

Fig. 28   Edging no. 1, plait with one picot

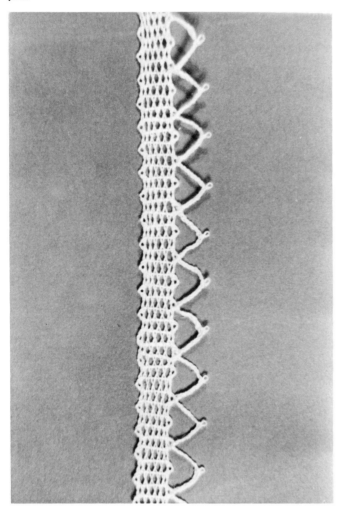

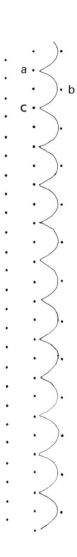

EDGING NO.1

Techniques used in working the edging – plait-with-picot (*page 26*), sewing in a pair of bobbins (*page 28*).

Method of working the edging

1. At *a* sew in two pairs of bobbins to the loop of the braid or the flower, etc.

2. Work a short plait to *b* where a RH picot is worked. Firm the threads and plait to *c*.

3. Sew in the LH pair of bobbins to the loop of the braid or flower, etc. Slide the second pair of bobbins through the loop in

the direction you are working. Keep the pairs in the right order and firm the threads.

4. You will see that alternate loops are used for the sewings. Complete the plait-with-picot edge and sew the pairs of bobbins into the loop at a to make the circle. Tie and cut off the threads.

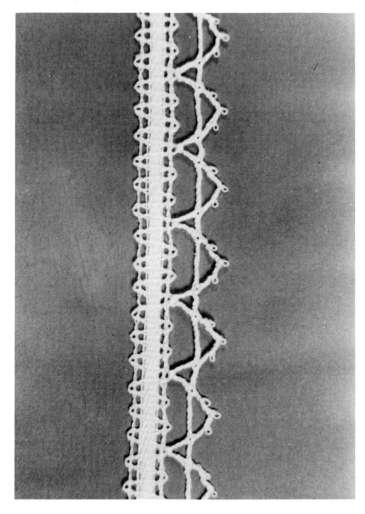

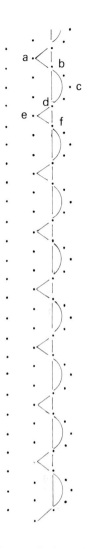

Fig. 29   Edging no.2, plaits with three picots on the outer plait

Photo 17b   Edging no.2, two plaits, one with three picots

EDGING NO.2

Techniques used to work the edging – plait-with-picot (*page 26*), windmill (*page 34*), sewing in a pair of bobbins (*page 28*). Make sure that four pairs of bobbins are fully wound with thread.

Method of working the edging

1. Into the loop of the braid at a sew in two pairs of bobbins and work a short plait to b. At b join in two more pairs of bobbins.

2. With the two RH pairs of bobbins work the plait-with-picots, from *b* and round to *d*. Leave them and with the LH set of two pairs of bobbins work the plait straight across to *d*.
3. At *d* join the four pairs of bobbins together with a windmill.
4. With the RH set of bobbins work a short plait to *f*. Leave them. With the LH set of bobbins work a short plait to *e*. Here make a sewing into the pinloop of the braid. The LH pair is sewn in and the RH pair is passed through the loop. Keep the pairs in order.
5. From *e* work a short plait to *f*, where the two sets of bobbins are joined with a windmill.
6. When the edging is complete, finally sew the pairs of bobbins into the loop at *a* and the two pairs into the loop at *b*. Tie and cut off the threads.

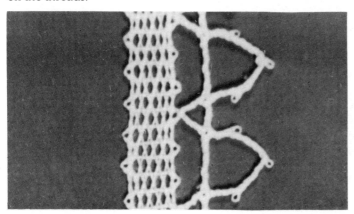

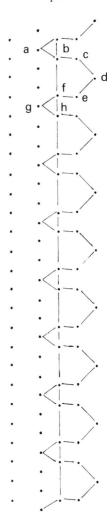

Photo 17c   Edging no.3, two plaits, one pointed with three picots

Fig. 30   Edging no.3, two plaits with three picots on the outer plait

EDGING NO.3

Techniques used in working the edging – plait-with-picot, windmill and sewing in a pair of bobbins.
Make sure that four pairs of bobbins are fully wound.

Method of working the edging

1. Into the loop of the braid at *a* sew in two pairs of bobbins and work a short plait to *b*. Join in two more pairs of bobbins.
2. With the RH set of two pairs of bobbins, plait to *c* where a RH picot is worked and again at *d* and *e*. Work a short plait to *f*.
3. With the LH two pairs of bobbins plait across to *f*, where the four pairs are joined with a windmill.
4. With the LH bobbins work a short plait to *g*. Here a sewing is made into the loop of the braid in the normal way. From *f* and *g* work short plaits to *h*, where they are joined with a windmill.
5. When the edging is complete, sew in and tie off the two pairs of bobbins into the loop at *a* and two pairs of bobbins into the pinloop at *b*.

WALKABOUT, 60/2 LINEN THREAD

Techniques used in the motif – h st, tallies (*page 26*), sewings, false plait (*page 32*), joining the braids together (*page 62*), no.1 edging and tying off several threads.

Method of working the motif

1. Prepare the pattern as previously explained.
2. Along the line at *a* put up five pins and hang two pairs of bobbins on to each pin, side by side.
3. Starting with the two RH pairs, work a d st. Using h st work towards the inner edge. Work the d st edge. Work the braid in a clockwise direction, noting where the sewings are worked at *b*, and the false plaits at *c*.
4. Upon reaching the starter pins, sew in the threads to the loops about the pins. Tie and cut off all the threads in the usual way.
5. Work the tallies.

The edging

Complete the motif by working edging no.1. Two picots have been used in the plait.

Fig. 31 Walkabout – a simple motif worked in half stitch braid and joined with false plaits and tallies

48

5

The fillings

Bruges Flower lace, one of the most popular Flemish laces, is noted for the fillings used to enhance the flowers, braids, leaves, scrolls and other artistic features. There are many fillings used in Flower lace, of which four have been selected and used in the designs found in the book. The fillings have been worked out mathematically on graph paper, using a compass and ruler. When braids, flowers and scrolls are used with fillings it is not always possible for the pinholes and the fillings to match accurately. So by moving the pinholes slightly, one way or the other, the two techniques will join successfully.

Take care when sewing in the threads. They must be sewn in at the correct pinloop so that the threads will lie at the correct angle. The same principle applies when sewing out the threads. Sew out one pair each time and leave them – rather than sew in, tie, and cut off. When all the pairs are sewn in, firm them, make a check to see that all is correct, then tie the threads and cut them off. This will allow you to unpick errors easily, should any threads be out of line.

Fill the bobbins with thread as it is difficult to join in another thread in a plait.

Each filling has its own characteristics, for example plaits-with-picots, cl st, h st twists and h st and buds as we know them. Notice the direction in which each filling is worked. Four small glassmats have been designed, each with a filling and a different braid. Each braid requires ten pairs of bobbins.

JOSEPHINE, FILLING NO.1, 60/2 LINEN (see photo 10)

Techniques used in working the motif – d st edge braid with ladder stitch, Dieppe ground (*page 24*), sewings (*page 32*),

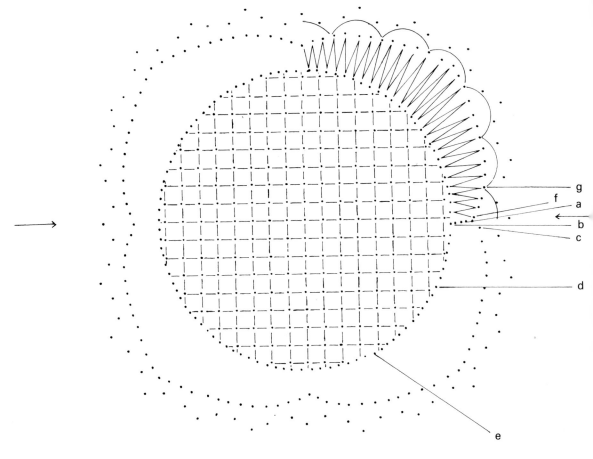

plait-with-picot, edging no.1 (*page 44*) and tying off all the threads (*page 35*).

Fig. 32   Josephine, filling no. 1, 60/2 linen, Dieppe ground

Method of working the motif

1. Prepare the pricking as previously explained.
2. Along the line at *a* put up five pins. Hang two pairs of bobbins on each pin, side by side.
3. At the outside edge work a d st with the two pairs of bobbins already about the pin. Using cl st work towards the inner edge *b*, where a d st edge is worked again. Firm the threads after each stitch.
4. Continue to work the braid in cl st. When the pin at *d* has been worked, start to work the 'ladder' in the braid. In the first three rows, twist the workers once when five pairs have been worked through in cl st. Firm all the threads. In the next three rows twist the workers twice, the next three rows, three times. Increase to four twists. Now reduce the twists gradually in reverse order as the braid progresses, a final single twist being made when *e* has been worked.

5. Work the braid in this manner, firming and shaping the threads. Finish the braid by working through all but the last pair. Sew the threads into the starter pinloops. Tie the threads in the usual way. Notice if any of the threads can be used for the fillings. Those not required can be cut off.

The filling – Dieppe ground

1. Wind the bobbins, winding a short length on to the empty bobbins to make a pair.
2. Sew three pairs of bobbins into the pinloops, above the ground marks, and two pairs into the RH pinloop. Put two twists on each pair of bobbins. Using the extreme RH pair work the first row of Dieppe ground, right to left. Sew the worker pair into the pinloop of the braid. Let them hang as a passive pair. Tension is a most important factor in this ground. The threads must be constantly firmed and the pins kept in line.
3. In the top section of the filling, pairs will be sewn in and left to hang as passive pairs when required. As the filling progresses the pairs will no longer be needed. Sew these pairs out and leave them. When the filling has been completed, sew in all the pairs. Firm them all again and tie each pair three times. Cut off the threads close to the lace.

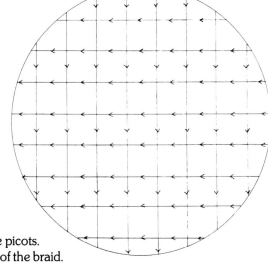

Fig. 33   Follow the arrows to work the Dieppe ground

The edging

1. Sew in two pairs at *g* and work a plait-with-three picots.
2. Sew the nearest pair of bobbins into the pinloop of the braid. Slide the other pair of bobbins through the loop, from back to front. Continue all round the edge and sew out two pairs of bobbins at *g*. Tie each pair of threads three times. Cut the threads close to the lace.

JOANNE, FILLING NO.2, 60/2 LINEN

Techniques used in working the motif – cl st (*page 22*), h st (*page*

Fig. 34   Joanne, filling no. 2, 60/2 linen

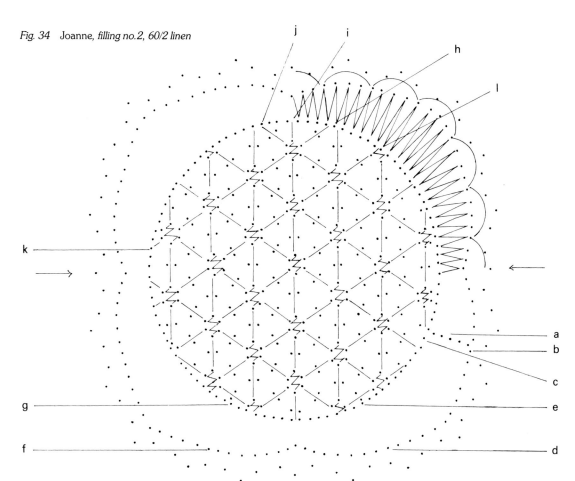

23), d st edge (*page 25*), plait-with-picots (*page 26*), sewings (*page 32*), h st buds (*page 53*), tying off several threads (*page 35*) and plait-with-picot edging no.1 (*page 44*).

Method of working the motif

1. Prepare the pricking as previously explained.
2. Along the line at *a* put up five pins. Hang two pairs of bobbins on each pin, side by side.
3. At *a* work a d st and work in h st to the inner edge. Firm all the passive threads, and work a d st edge at *c*.
4. Continue to work the braid in h st with d st edges, until d has been worked. Work a row of d st to the inner edge. Firm and shape the passive threads.
5. Work the next section in cl st. Work a row of d st, *f* to *g* to divide the section. Firm and shape the passive threads again. Complete the braid in this order, keeping the d st edges.
6. Firm and shape the passive threads. Sew each pair of threads into the starter pinloops, one pair sewn into one loop. Tie off the threads in the usual way. Cut the threads close to the lace with the lace scissors.

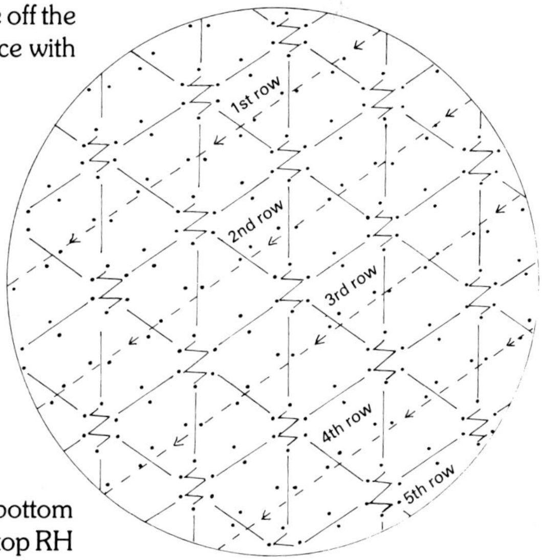

Fig. 35 *Follow the numbered rows to work the half stitch buds and plait-with-picots*

Method of working the filling

This filling is worked in a diagonal direction, top right to bottom left. In each row sew the bobbins into the pinloops at the top RH edge. Sew out the threads at the bottom LH edge. You will see from the diagram the number of rows to be worked.

1. Start at *h*, *i* and *j* by sewing two pairs of bobbins into each of the pinloops. Work three plaits with picots.
2. Work the buds in h st and put the pairs to one side for use again in the same row and the row below.
3. Continue to sew two pairs of bobbins into the pinloops of the braid. Work the plaits-with-picots and the h st buds in a diagonal direction. Put aside the pairs for use in the next row.
4. When *k* is reached two pairs are sewn out. Return to the top RH edge and start to work the second row. Start by working a small part of the bud at *l*.

5. Complete the diagonal row, sewing out threads where necessary into the pinloops of the braid. Finish the filling and sew in all the threads. Firm all the threads which have been sewn in, and ensure that a good line has been made. Tie each pair three times and cut off the threads close to the lace.

The edging

The plait with picot edge is worked similarly to the one in the Josephine motif.

JASMINE, FILLING NO.3, 60/2 LINEN

Techniques used in this motif – d st edge (*page 38*), sewings (*page 32*), windmill (*page 34*), plait with picot edging No.1 (*page 44*) and h st vein (*page 80*).

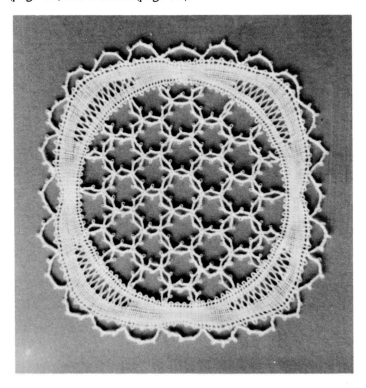

Photo 20   Filling no.3, plait-with-picot

Method of working the motif

1. Prepare the pricking as already explained.
2. Along the line at *a* put up five pins and hang two pairs of bobbins on each pin.
3. At the inner edge *b*, work a d st edge with the two pairs about the pin. Work in cl st to the outer edge *c*, and work the d st edge. Firm and shape the passive threads. Work a short length of braid

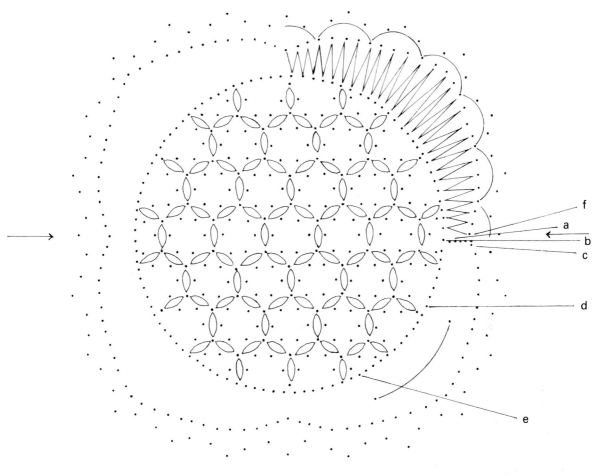

Fig. 36 Jasmine, *filling no.3, 60/2 linen*

in this way. Shape the threads to follow the line of the outside edge.

4. When the pin at *d* has been worked, start to work the h st vein. Cl st through two pairs, twist the next pair of threads and the worker pair once. Using these two pairs work a h st.

5. Cl st through four pairs and work the d st edge. Firm and shape the threads to follow the line of the outside edge so that they do not allow the h st vein to take up too much space.

6. Return to the inner edge in cl st working through four pairs of threads. Twist the workers once and work a h st. Firm, pull down and shape the threads. Finish working the vein at *e*.

7. Complete the braid working the h st veins. When *f* is reached sew the threads into the starter loops. Tie the threads in the usual way and cut off the threads close to the lace.

The filling

When working this filling, the threads should not be sewn in and cut off unnecessarily. Study the diagram and you will see that there are a series of numbers, showing the direction for working

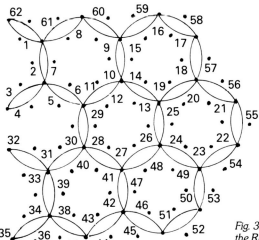

Fig. 37 *Follow the numbered route. Note the RH edge of the filling is worked last*

the rows. At the RH edge notice that the plaits and picots are not worked until the area of the filling has been worked fully. This does away with unnecessary sewings, tyings and cut-offs. The route for working the filling must be worked out before starting to work it. Look at the technical drawing and you will see that the:

1st row is worked L-R, 1 to 21
2nd row is worked R-L, 22 to 32
3rd row is worked L-R, 33 to 52. The completion row is worked 53 to 62.

The edging

The plait-with-picot edging is worked similarly to the one used in the Josephine motif.

JEANNE, FILLING NO.4, 60/2 LINEN

Techniques used in the motif – cl st, h st, d st edge braid and plait-with-picot edging no.1.

Method of working the motif

1. Prepare the pricking as previously explained.
2. Along the line at a put up five pins. Hang two pairs of bobbins on to each pin, side by side.
3. At the inner edge work a d st with the two pairs of bobbins about the pin at b. Using cl st work towards the outer edge. Work the d st edge at c.
4. Work a small section of the braid in cl st until the d st edge at d has been completed. Work a row of d st to the outer edge. Work the d st edge. Firm and shape the passive threads.
5. Each section is worked alternately in cl st and h st, separated

Photo 21　Filling no. 4, plait-with-picot

Fig. 38　Jeanne, filling no. 4, 60/2 linen

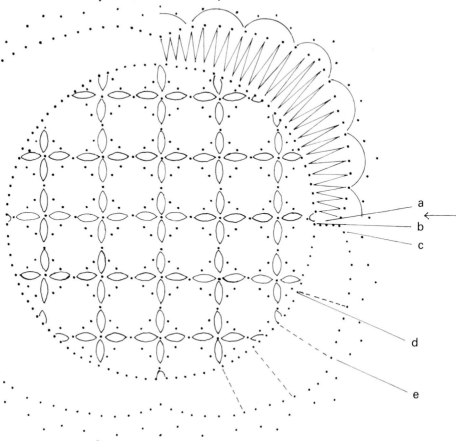

a

b

c

d

e

by a row of d st. Work from the inner to the outer edge. At *e* the section will change again.

6. Finally work a row of cl st to the inner edge and join the braid in the usual way.

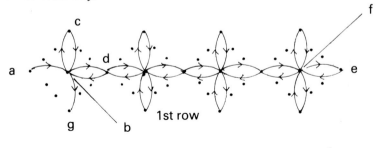

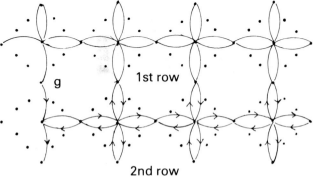

Fig. 39   Filling no.3 is worked with four bobbins. Follow the arrows

The filling

1. Wind two pairs of bobbins fully, so as to avoid making a join in a plait.

2. At *a* sew two pairs of bobbins into the pinloop of the braid or flower. Work a plait-with-picot to *b*. Put up a pin between the two pairs of bobbins.

3. Turn the pillow. Work a second plait-with-picot to *c*. Make a sewing into the pinloop of the braid.

4. Turn the pillow and work the plait-with-picot to *b* and place the two pairs of bobbins about the pin already there.

5. Turn the pillow and work the plait-with-picot to *d*. Place a pin between the two pairs. Repeat *a* to *d* along the row. Make a sewing into the braid at *e*.

6. Turn the pillow. Work the plait-with-picot to *f*. Place the pairs of bobbins around the pin for a third time. Follow the arrows and when *f* is reached again, remove the pin, and make a sewing through all the loops about the pin. Repeat the plait-with-picots along the row until *g* is worked.

7. Now start to work the second row. Note that the plaits-with picots at the LH edge are left unworked. When all the rows are finished, these plaits-with picots are completed and the pairs are then sewn out at *a*.

The edging

The plait-with-picot edging is worked similarly to the one used in the Josephine motif.

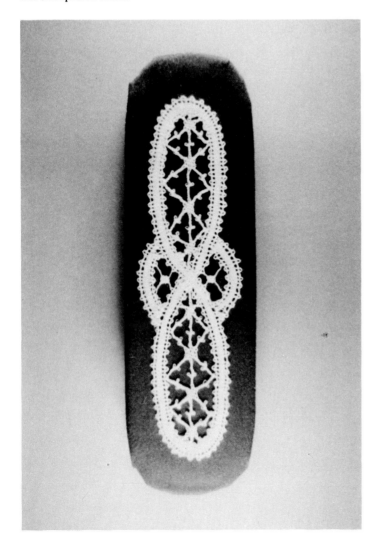

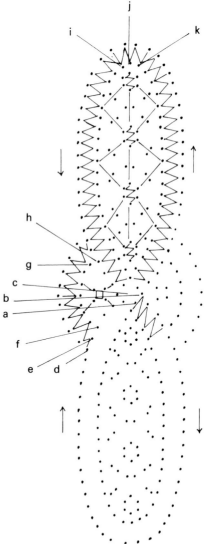

Photo 22   A clothes brush, using braid no.3 and filling no.2

Fig. 40   The Trail. Cloth stitch braid and filling no.3 are used together in this motif which is mounted on the back of a clothes brush

THE TRAIL (A BRUSH), 60/2 LINEN

Techniques used in this motif – cl st, d st edge braid, crossing of two braids, joining of two braids, tally and filling no.2.

Method of working the motif

1. Prepare the pricking as previously explained.
2. Along the line at *a* put up three pins and hang on two pairs of bobbins on each pin, and one extra pair on the centre pin.

3. Starting from the inner edge work a d st edge. Using cl st work to the outer edge and complete the d st edge. Continue to work the braid in this manner, noting where the b st are worked, *i*, *j* and *k*.

4. When the first loop of the braid has been completed and the starter pins are reached, work the first d st of the edge stitch. Remove the pin and using the worker pair make a sewing into the first pair of loops. Firm the threads. Twist the edge pair once, and complete the d st edge. Work across to the other edge and work the edge stitch. Repeat this until all the pairs of loops have been joined.

5. Complete the braid, crossing one braid over the other at *c*, sewing the threads into the starter loops. Tie off the threads in the usual way, and cut them close to the lace.

6. Work the small braids at each side, by sewing in two pairs of bobbins into the pinloop at *d*, and one pair into the braid between *d* and *e*. Using the two RH pairs work a d st edge and cl st through the pair sewn into the braid.

7. Cl st back to the outer edge and work the d st edge.

8. Sew in one pair of bobbins at *e*, two pairs of bobbins into the braid to the left of *e*, and one pair of bobbins at *f*.

9. Using cl st work the small braid, noticing where the b st is worked.

10 .When *g* has been worked, one pair of bobbins can be sewn out at *h*, and two pairs sewn out into the edge of the braid. Follow the worker line carefully and finish working the braid. The remaining pairs are sewn out just as they were sewn in. Tie off the threads in the usual way and cut them off close to the lace.

11. The filling is worked next, working from the top edge to the centre, and from the centre to the bottom edge. Work the tallies.

12. Remove all the pins. Press the motif lightly on the WS and tack it on to a piece of silk, taffeta or similar fabric. Using a fine thread, matching the motif, catch-stitch the lace to the fabric. Mount on the back of the brush.

13. Work the d st edge braid no.3, so that it will fit firmly round the edge of the brush. Join the braid into a circle and sew it into place.

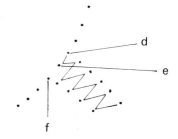

Fig. 41   Setting up and working the two small braids

6

The flowers of Bruges Flower lace

As the title of the book implies, the flowers are the main part of the lace. They are of many shapes, requiring individual techniques and I have selected ten of them for you to work. Their main use is of course in the 'piece' lace, but they can be used as an attractive insertion in dresses, blouses, children's wear and aprons. Each individual flower may be used on its own, under a paper-weight, a pin-cushion, or in the lid of a trinket-box. They can be arranged to make a very attractive picture. Each flower is worked in 60/2 linen.

Care should be taken when working the lace to allow the passive threads to follow the curve of the outer edge of the petal. There is a great danger of pulling the passive threads straight so the edge of the flower becomes loose and unsightly. After each row has been worked the passive threads should be shaped and firmed carefully. The petals of each flower may be separated from the other in one of the following ways:

a. One row of d st worked from the outer to the inner edge.
b. Plaits.
c. Two twists made on each pair of passives.

FLOWER NO.1

The simplest flower will be worked first.
Techniques used in the motif – cl st, h st, d st edge, b st (*page 32*), filling no.1 (*page 49*), d st (*page 25*) and joining into a circle (*page 62*).

Method of working the motif

1. Along the line at *a* put up five pins. Hang two pairs of bobbins on to each pin.

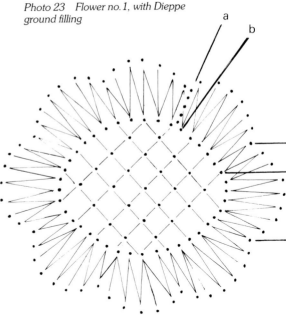

Photo 23   Flower no. 1, with Dieppe
ground filling

Fig. 42   Flower no. 1

2. Using the first pair of bobbins, work in cl st to the outer edge.
Work a d st edge. Work back to the inner edge through all but
one pair.

3. At b work the d st edge.

4. Return to the outer edge in cl st and complete the d st edge.
Notice that where three lines meet at the next pinhole on the
inner edge, a b st is worked. When working in cl st, twist the
worker pair twice, when working in h st put an extra twist on the
worker pair. Pass the worker pair behind the last pin and under
the edge pair. Continue to work to the outer edge. Complete the
working of this petal in cl st.

5. When the edge stitch at c has been completed, twist each pair
of passive threads. Work a row of d st to the point marked d.
Work the d st edge. Firm the passives.

6. From e work the second petal in h st. Note where the b st are
worked. Firm and shape the passives.

7. Work a row of d st to the inner edge. Do not pull the passive
threads.

8. Work all the petals, alternating them in cl st and h st. Firm and
shape the passive threads so that a neat and well-shaped petal
results. When the d st at a has been worked, twist each pair of
passives and work a row of d st towards the inner edge.

9. All the threads must now be sewn into the starter pinloops.
There will be two loops about each pin. Sew a pair of threads
into each loop, each loop corresponding to a pair of bobbins.
Using a fine crochet hook, slide the hook through the pinloop
and catch the thread on the hook. Pull the hook and thread back

through the pinloop and slide the other bobbin into the loop. Firm the threads and lay them to the back of the work. Sew in the next pair into the next loop. Remove the pins and repeat the sewings. Complete the joining of the petals into a circle. Firm all the threads and tie as described. One or two pairs near the inner edge will be used for the filling. Cut off the threads close to the lace.

The filling

The filling used is Dieppe ground as described in filling no. 1.

FLOWER NO.2

This flower has six petals, forming a simple design and featuring another centre filling. The petals may be worked in h st or cl st or alternately in cl st/h st.
Techniques used in the motif – cl st, h st, d st edge, plait-with-picot, d st, joining into a circle and b st.

Fig. 43   Flower no.2

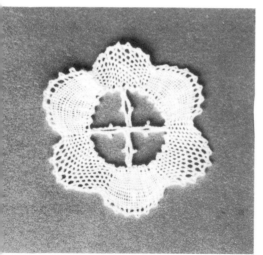

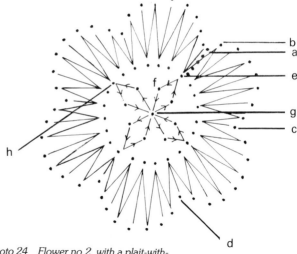

Photo 24   Flower no.2, with a plait-with-picot filling

Method of working the motif

1. Along a line at *a* put up five pins and hang two pairs of bobbins on each pin. Using the first pair start to work a row of cl st to the outer edge. Work the d st edge, remembering to twist the worker pair an extra time before putting up the pin.
2. When the d st edge has been worked at *b*, return in cl st to the inner edge. Work the d st edge, and note that when returning to this pinhole for a second time, a b st is worked. Work the b st and return to the outer edge in either h st or cl st, whichever you have chosen to work. Firm and shape the passives to follow the

outer curve of the petal. When c has been worked, separate the
petals with a row of d st worked towards the inner edge.

3. Work the second petal in either cl st or h st. When the pinhole
at d has been worked, separate the petals with a row of d st.
Continue to work the petals stopping at e in the last one. The
centre filling can be worked in the following way before the last
petal is completed. The filling is worked in an anti-clockwise
direction.

1. At e work a d st and put up a pin.
2. Work a plait to f with the two edge pairs. Work a picot.
   Continue the plait to g. Place the pairs about a pin.
3. Work a plait with picot to h. Take out the pin at h and sew in
   the LH pair and pass the other pair through the loop in the
   direction you are working. Replace the pin. Firm the threads.
   Continue to work the plait-with-picot back to g.
4. Place the pairs about the pin.
5. Work the other groups of plaits with picots by following the
   arrowed lines until g is worked for the last time. Remove the
   pin at g and sew through all the loops about the pin. Slide the
   other pair through the loop. Put the pin back into the hole and
   firm the threads. Complete the last plait-with-picot to e. Sew
   in the RH pair and slide the other pair through the loop. Work
   a d st to bring the two pairs used for the plait back into the
   petal. Finish the petal and join the passive threads into their
   corresponding pinloops. Tie off in the way described. Cut off
   the pairs one at a time.

FLOWER NO.3

This flower has six petals and introduces one of the most
attractive techniques used in Bruges Flower lace, a raised edge.

*Photo 25   Flower no.3, with a raised edge
and Dieppe ground filling*

Fig. 44   Flower no.3

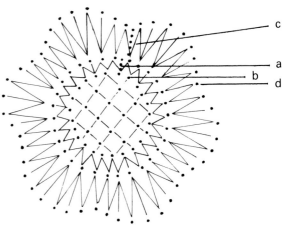

A similar technique will be found in Duchesse and Honiton lace (*see photo 4b*). The inner circle is worked first and the petals are attached to it by means of sewings. In order to keep the work neat, the starting line of both the inner circle and the petals should be kept in a continuous line. Pairs from the inner circle are used to work the filling and join the inner circle and the petals together.

Techniques used in the motif – cl st, h st, d st, d st edge, four-about-the-pin edge, single and double sewings in a raised edge, filling no.1, joining into a circle and tying off a number of threads.

The inner circle

1. Along the line at *a* put up three pins and hang two pairs on each pin. Using the two RH pairs, work a cl st with two twists on each. Cl st to the inner edge, where a d st edge is worked at *b*.
2. Cl st to the outer edge and work the four-about-the-pin edge. Firm the passive threads, do not pull them.
3. Complete the inner circle and when the last pin has been worked, take the worker to the outer edge. Remove the pin and join the inner circle into a circle. One or two of the pairs near the inner edge should be used to work the filling and one pair at the RH edge should be used to work the petals.

The petals

1. Along the line at *c* put up five pins and hang on six pairs of bobbins. A centre pin will take the extra pair. Starting at the inner edge, and using the pair from the inner circle, work a row of cl st to the outer edge. Work the d st edge and return in cl st to the inner edge. Remove the pin from the edge of the inner circle, next to the tying-off line, and make a sewing into the first bar of the first pinloop.
2. Where three lines meet at the one pinhole, use the second bar to act as a b st. Firm the threads so that they do not slip, and work back to the outer edge. When using cl st and before making a sewing, twist the workers once. This twist is already there when working in h st.
3. Cl st to the outer edge, and work the d st edge. Work back to the inner edge. Remove the next pin and sew into the first of the two bars. Firm the threads and replace the pin. Using the second bar of this pinloop will act as a b st.
3. Complete the petal, noting where the b st are worked. When only one sewing is made, take the crocket hook under both bars to make the loop. When *d* has been worked, work a row of d st towards the inner circle, and make a sewing into the next pinloop, taking up both bars in the sewing. Complete all the petals, remembering to divide them with a row of d st worked

from the outer edge to the inner edge. Examine the pricking to ascertain whether one bar or two bars are used to make the sewing.

4. Finally, before joining the petals together, twist all the passive threads once and then work the row of d st. Make the sewings into the starter loops. Firm all the threads and finally tie them in the usual way. Cut off the threads close to the lace.

The filling

Now work filling no.1 in the centre of the flower, using the two pairs from the inner circle.

FLOWER NO.4

This flower repeats the techniques of an inner circle, the petals and the plait and picot filling. The inner circle and the petals are joined by a new technique, a false plait. The petals may be worked in cl st or h st or worked alternately in cl st and h st. The petals are separated by a row of d st.

Techniques used in the motif – cl st, b st, d st, d st edge, plait-with-picot filling, false plait and joining into a circle.

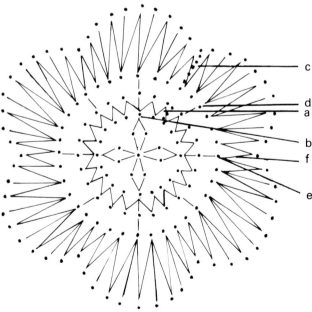

Fig. 45   Flower no.4

Photo 26a   Flower no.4, with an inner circle and petals, joined with false plaits

Method of working the motif
THE INNER CIRCLE
1. Along the line at *a* put up three pins and hang on six pairs of bobbins side by side. Work the inner circle as in flower no.3 but with d st edges. Notice where the b st are worked. The centre filling is worked when *b* is reached, as in flower no.2.
2. Work the filling in an anti-clockwise direction. To improve the appearance of the plaits, keep the same number of stitches in each section of the plait. Firm the threads.
3. Finish the inner circle in the usual way. Remember to join the circle by sewing one pair of threads into one loop around the starter pin.

THE PETALS
1. Along the line at *c*, put up six pins and hang on 12 pairs of bobbins, side by side. Work a row of cl st to the outer edge. Work the d st edge and return to the inner edge in cl st, note where the b st are worked. Work the d st edge. Continue to work the petal until *d* is reached. Work the false plait, cl st to the outer edge and work the edge stitch. Return to the inner edge and work the b st.
2. Complete the petal, and at *f* work a row of d st towards the inner edge. At *e* work a second false plait. Work back to the outer edge and work the d st edge. Firm all the passive threads and shape them to follow the curve of the outer edge. Do not pull them.
3. Complete the petals in this way, using cl st or h st as you wish. Take care to work the b st and the false plaits.
4. Join the first and the last petal as already described in flower no.1.
5. Firm all the threads. Tie them off in the usual way and cut the threads close to the lace.

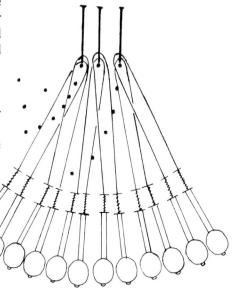

Fig. 46   Side by side hanging on of six pairs of bobbins

Photo 26b   Flower no.4, used to decorate a pincushion, edged with braid-on-a-footing

*Photo 27   Flower no.5, with eight petals, a
raised edge and plait-with-picot filling*

Fig. 47   Flower no.5

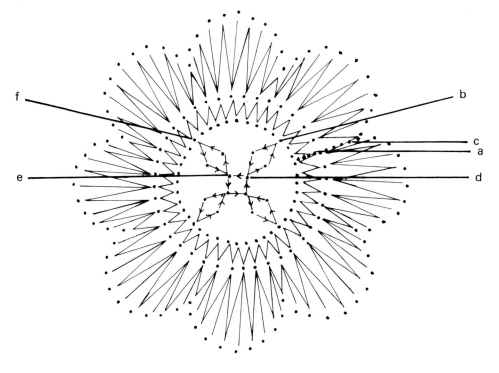

FLOWER NO.5

This flower is similar to flower no.3. There are eight petals, which should be worked in h st, or cl st, or alternately in h st and cl st. There is a new centre filling and the instructions will be given in due course.

The inner circle is worked first in cl st, and the petals are joined to it by the raised edge technique.

The inner circle

Techniques used in the motif – cl st, h st, d st edge, raised edge sewings, plait-with-picots, sewings, d st, tying off a number of threads and joining into a circle.

Method of working the motif

1. Along the line at *a* put up four pins and hang on eight pairs of bobbins, side by side. Work the inner circle as described in flower no.3, but without the b st.
2. At *b* start to work the filling, using the two edge pairs. The filling is worked in an anti-clockwise direction. Work the small plait-with-picot to *d* and put up a pin between the pairs. Work a small plait to *e* and put a pin between the two pairs.
3. Work a plait-with-picot to *f*. Remove the pin and make a sewing into the pinloop of the braid. Sew in the RH pair and pass the LH pair through the loop. Replace the pin. Firm the threads. Work a plait-with-picot back to *e*. Remove the pin and make a sewing into the thread about the pin. Replace the pin and firm the threads. The short plaits join the plait-with-picots.
4. Complete the filling round to *b*, sewing into the pinloop, and work a d st. Finish working the inner circle and make the join as described in flower no.1, one pair of threads into one loop. Tie off the threads in the usual way and cut them off close to the lace.

The petals

1. Along the line at *c* put up five pins and hang on ten pairs of bobbins, side by side. These petals are worked as described in flower no.3. Use the pair from the inner circle as workers and work a row of cl st to the outer edge.
2. Work the d st edge and work back to the inner circle. Make a sewing, using the first bar of the first pinloop, all the bars will be used to work the stitches. When using cl st and before working the sewing, twist the workers once.
3. Complete the petals as described in flower no.3. Join the last petal to the first petal in the usual way. Tie all the threads and cut them off close to the lace.

Photo 28   Flower no.6, oval in shape,
with inner circle and petals, joined with
false plaits, and plait-with-picot filling

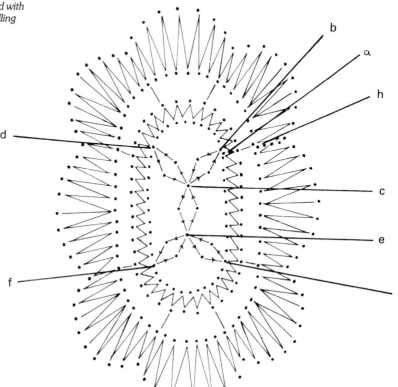

Fig. 48   Flower no.6

FLOWER NO.6

The shape of this flower now moves away from the traditional round shape of the flowers. It is worked using the same techniques found in flower no. 4, an inner circle and the petals, a false plait, and a new centre filling which will be explained. The filling is worked before the inner circle is completed, using the two pairs from *b*. This filling is worked in an anti-clockwise direction.

Techniques used in the motif – cl st (*page 22*), h st (*page 23*), d st (*page 25*), d st edge (*page 38*), plait-with-picot (*page 26*), false plait (*page 32*) and joining into a circle (*page 62*).

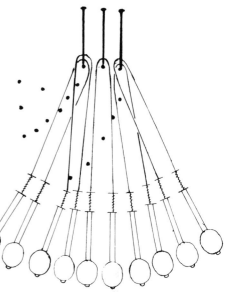

Fig. 49   The hanging on of bobbins side by side and a single pair of bobbins

Method of working the motif

1. To refresh your memory, always set up the inner circle and the petals in a continuous line.
2. Along the line at *a* put up three pins and hang on five pairs of bobbins. Follow the instructions for the inner circle in flower no.4, but no b st are used. Start working the filling when the pinhole at *b* has been reached.
3. Work the d st, put up the pin between the pairs.
4. Work a plait-with-picot to *c*, put up the pin between the two pairs. Work a plait-with-picot back to *d*. Remove the pin and sew in the nearest pair into the pinloop of the braid. Slide the other pair through the loop. Replace the pin. Firm the threads and work a plait-and-picot to *c*. Put up a pin between the pairs. Work a plait-with-picot to *e* and put up a pin between the two pairs of bobbins.
5. Work a plait-with-picot to *f*. Remove the pin and work a sewing into the pinloop. Replace the pin. Work back to *e* and place the two pairs of bobbins around the pin at *e*. Work a plait-with-picot to *g*, where a sewing is made into the pinloop of the braid.
6. Work a plait-with-picot back to *e*. Remove the pin and make a sewing through all the loops about the pin. Replace the pin and firm the threads.
7. Work to *c*, remove the pin and make another sewing through all the loops about the pin. Replace the pin and firm the threads. Work the last plait-with-picot to *b*. Remove the pin, and make the sewing. Replace the pin. Finish working the inner circle.
8. When a sewing has been worked, untangle the threads, and make sure that they are flat and firm before continuing to work a further plait.

The petals

1. Along the line at *h* put up four pins and hang on nine pairs of bobbins. Using the first pair of bobbins work in cl st to the outer edge. Work the d st edge. With the help of the instructions given for flower no.4, complete the petals. Notice where the b st and the false plaits are worked.

2. Join the first petal to the last petal as already described, sewing one pair of threads into one loop. Do not pull the threads tight when making the sewings.

FLOWER NO.7

You will notice that each petal is separated by plaits. The petals may be worked in one of the combinations of stitches: all h st; all cl st; or alternate cl st and h st. This flower has a raised edge. A tally is worked in the centre.

Techniques used in the motif – cl st, h st, d st edge, four-about-the-pin edge, d st, plaits, tally, b st, raised edge sewings, joining a circle and tying off threads.

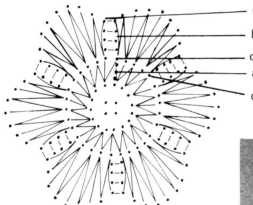

Fig. 50   Flower no.7

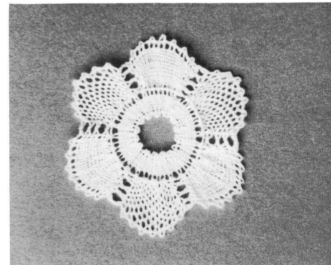

Photo 29   Flower no. 7, with a raised edge and six petals joined with short plaits

Method of working the motif

1. Along the line at *a* put up four pins and hang on six pairs of bobbins. Follow the instructions for the inner circle used in flower no.3. The outer edge of this circle has a four-about-the-pin edge. The edge is raised.
2. Join the circle, one pair of threads being sewn into one loop. Tie off the threads, and place one pair at the outer edge to one side, to be used in the petals.

The petals

1. Along the line at *b* put up four pins. On the LH pin, hang on one pair, and two pairs on to the other three pins. Bring the pair from the inner circle and place round the first pin. Twist each pair once and work a row of d st to the inner edge.
2. Make a sewing at *c*, remembering to take the hook under both bars. B st are needed and each bar of each loop will be required on the next three pins, and both bars of the last pin. When using cl st twist the workers once before making the sewing. When h st is used the twist is already there. Sew the LH thread into the pinloop and slide the other thread through the loop.
3. Firm the threads and shape them to follow the line of the outer curve. Work back to the outer edge and work the d st edge. Complete the petal, note where the sewings are made. Finish each petal by working a row of d st to the outer edge.
4. The small plaits which divide the petals must be made now. Use the pairs on either side of each pin to make two or three plait stitches across to the corresponding pin of the next petal.
5. Starting from the outer edge, work a row of d st across to the inner circle and make a sewing as before.
6. Work all the petals, and when the last pin has been put up at *e*, put the pins between the pairs of bobbins, ready to work the plaits across to the starter loops. Work the small plaits, and sew each pair from the plait into the corresponding pinloop. Tie off each pair of threads three times.

FLOWER NO.8

This flower is very similar to flower no.7. The same techniques are used in both flowers. There are, however, only five sections in the flower, two worked in cl st and three worked in h st, each section divided by plaits.

Techniques used in the motif – cl st, h st, d st, d st edge, b st, four-about-the-pin edge, plaits and raised edge sewings.

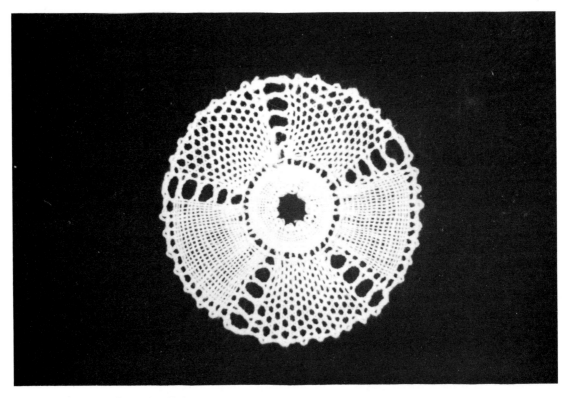

Photo 30 Flower no.8, a five-petalled
flower, separated with small plaits, around
a raised edge inner circle

Fig. 51 Flower no.8

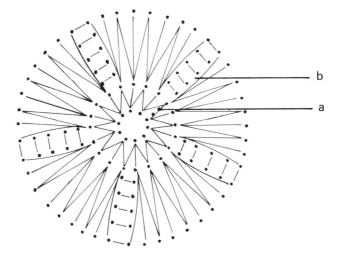

Method of working the motif
INNER CIRCLE

1. Along the line at *a* put up four pins. Hang two pairs on to each
pin. Follow the instructions for the inner circle in flower no.3.
Complete the circle. Join the threads to the starter loops.

2. Tie off the threads in the usual way, leaving one pair at the RH side to be used in the flower. Cut off the other threads close to the lace.

THE PETALS

1. The petals are exactly the same as those in flower no. 7. If you have worked the flowers in a progressive order you will have no problems with this technique.

2. Along the line at *b* put up five pins and hang on nine pairs of bobbins, remembering to place the pair from the inner circle around the first pin.

3. There are five petals in the flower. Two are worked in cl st and three in h st.

4. Join the plaits to the starter loops as described in flower no. 7. Tie off each pair of threads three times each. Cut off the threads close to the lace.

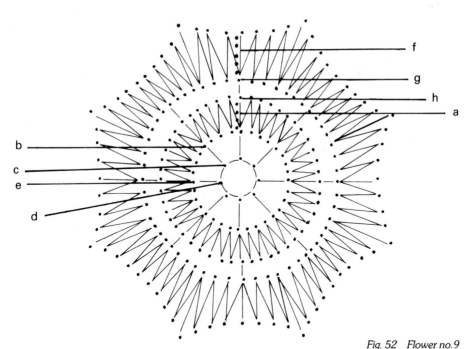

Fig. 52   Flower no. 9

FLOWER NO. 9

Here you will find another flower with an unusual shape. The techniques used in working this flower may be found in flower no. 6. The inner circle is worked in cl st, and the petals are

worked in h st. This flower is known as the Chinese Rose. A new centre filling will be introduced.

Techniques used in the motif – h st, cl st, b st, d st edge, false plait, plaits and joining into a circle.

Method of working the motif

INNER CIRCLE

1. Along the line at *a* put up four pins. Hang two pairs of bobbins on each pin. Now follow the instructions for the inner circle of flower no. 4 as far as pin *b*.
2. This filling is also worked before completing the inner circle. Work the edge stitch at *b* and using the LH pair of the edge pairs, twist them three times. Put up a pin at *c*, hang on one pair of bobbins. Using these two pairs, work a cl st, pin, cl st at *c*. Work in an anti-clockwise direction.
3. Plait to *d* and put up a pin in the centre of the plait. Work the false plait to *e* and back to *d*. Finish the filling, using the plaits and false plaits, until *c* is reached. Sew out one pair of bobbins at *c*. Tie them off carefully and lay them to the back of the work. Cut them off upon completion of the inner circle.
4. From the back of the false plait, using a crochet hook, ease through one of the threads and slide the other thread through the loop. Ease the threads towards the inner circle. Sew in at *b*, work a d st and finish working the inner circle.
5. Join the circle in the usual way. Tie off all the threads and cut them close to the lace.

THE PETALS

1. Along the line at *f* put up five pins and hang on two pairs on each pin. From *g* work a row of h st to the outer edge. Work the d st edge and return to the inner edge which is worked in a d st edge.
2. Work the flower in continuous h st, noting where the b st and the false plaits are worked.
3. Join the threads to the starter pinloops, one pair of threads to one pinloop. Tie off all the threads and cut them close to the lace.

FLOWER NO.10

This flower is very attractive and after working the other flowers it will be found easy to work. The eight petals of the flower are separated by plaits. Each petal starts and finishes with a row of d st from the outer to the inner edge. The petals are worked in any of the already mentioned stitches. The edge of the inner

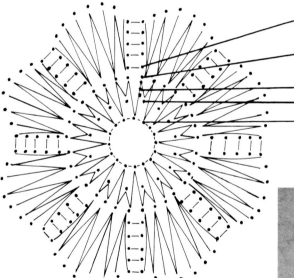

Fig. 53 Flower no.10

Photo 32 Flower no.10, a raised edge, inner circle extended to another inner circle. Eight petals separated with short plaits

circle is raised, and the inner edge of this section is broken by an extension of the edge to another circle.

Techniques used in the motif – cl st, h st, d st, d st edge, plaits, raised edge sewings, twists, four-about-the-pin edge and tying off several threads.

Method of working the motif

INNER CIRCLE

1. Along the line at *a* put up three pins and hang two pairs on each pin.
2. Start to work from the outer edge by working a cl st with two twists on each pair. Put up the pin to the left of the two pairs. Use the LH pair as workers.
3. Cl st through four pairs, twist the workers twice. Put up a pin at *b* and return to the outer edge in cl st.
4. Work the four-about-the-pin edge. Work through four pairs in cl st. Twist the workers three times. Hang in another pair at *c* and use it to work a d st edge at *c*.
5. Twist the workers twice, three twists altogether.
6. Work in cl st through four pairs. Work the four-about-the-pin edge. Finish working the inner circle in this way, until all the pinholes are worked. Join the circle in the usual way. Tie off the threads, putting aside one pair to be used in the petals. Cut off the threads close to the lace.

THE PETALS

1. Along the line at *d* put up a pin next to the inner circle. On this pin hang the pair from the inner circle and one more pair.
2. Put up four pins to the right of *d*. Hang two pairs of bobbins on each pin. Put a twist on each pair.
3. Close the edge pin with a d st, and work a row of d st to the inner edge. Remove the pin at *e*. Make a sewing into the first bar about the pin. A twist will already be on the worker pair. Replace the pin. Firm the threads. Remember that when working a b st use the second of the two bars. It will be necessary to use each bar at each pinloop.
4. Upon completion of the petal, a twist is made on each pair and a row of d st is worked from the outer to the inner edge. Put the pin up between the two pairs and work the small plaits across to the next petal. Put the pins up between the pairs ready to work the petal.
5. Work a row of d st from the outer to the inner edge and work a sewing as before, remembering to cross the workers once when using cl st before working the sewing.
6. When all the petals are worked, complete the small plaits and join them to the first petal by sewing them into the starter pinloops. Replace the pins, and tie off each pair three times. Cut them close to the lace.

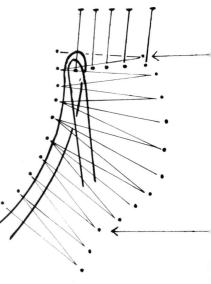

Fig. 54 Hanging on pairs of bobbins side by side. The arrows indicate the direction of the row of double stitches

7

The leaves and scrolls

The leaves used in the lace introduce many new techniques. They are worked as a single leaf, two leaves joined together at the base, and three leaves joined to form a clover leaf or 'Drieblad' leaf. The d st edge is used at the edges of the leaves. One half is worked in cl st, and the other half in h st. The centre vein is raised, and a four-about-the-pin edge is worked at this point. The cl st is worked to the top centre pin of the leaf, and the leaf then finished in h st.

A SINGLE LEAF, 60/2 LINEN

Techniques used in the motif — cl st, d st, d st edge, braid no.3 and hanging in a pair.

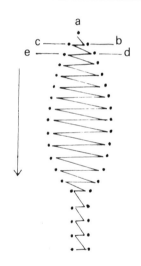

Fig. 55   A single leaf

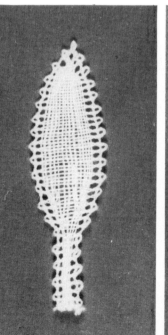
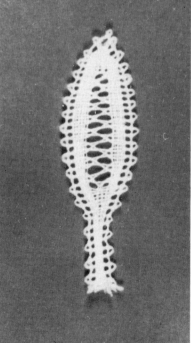

Photo 33a   Single leaf

Photo 33b   Single leaf with half stitch vein

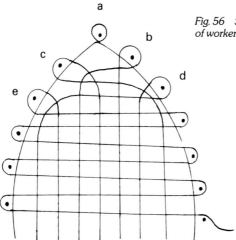

a
b
c
d
e

Fig. 56   Setting up a leaf. Note the change of worker

Fig. 57   Put two twists on the right hand pair

Method of working the motif

1. Prepare the pricking as previously explained.

2. At *a* put up a pin. Hang two pairs of bobbins on the pin. Make two twists on the RH pair. Close the pin with a d st. These two pairs are used to work the edge stitch of the leaf.

3. At *b* put up a pin. Hang two pairs of bobbins on the pin. Make two twists on the RH pair. Using the RH pair from the centre pin work through both of these pairs in d st. Leave them.

4. At *c* put up a pin. Hang on two pairs of bobbins. Make two twists on the RH pair. Work both of these pairs through the LH centre pair in d st. Allow both of these to hang as passive pairs. Leave them.

5. Using the RH pair from pin *b*, cl st through three pairs. Allow the worker pair to hang as a passive pair. At *d* put up a pin. Hang on two pairs of bobbins as before. Make two twists on the RH pair. Using the RH pair which has travelled from the centre pin at *a*, work a d st through both pairs.

6. Using the LH pair from *c*, cl st through four pairs. Leave them.

7. At *e* put up a pin. Hang on two pairs of bobbins. Make two twists on the RH pair. Using the LH pair from the centre pin at *a*, work a d st through both of these pairs.

8. Using the RH pair from *d*, work through six pairs of bobbins in cl st. Allow the worker pair to hang as a passive pair. The LH pair from *e* now becomes the worker pair.

Continue to work the leaf in cl st, working a d st edge. The centre of the leaf may be decorated with twists made on the workers. Starting at the centre, make one twist on the workers, with an equal number of pairs either side. There should be the

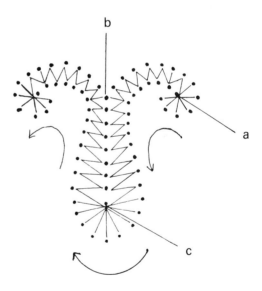

same number of threads at each side of the twists and it will
therefore be necessary to hang in another pair. On the next row,
in the centre, work two twists on the worker pair. When the leaf
narrows, finally work one twist on the worker pair. Reduce the
threads to six pairs. Work the stem, tie off the threads. Firm them
and cut off the threads close to the lace.

There are two other fillings which may be used on this leaf, ie,
a h st vein worked by using one h st in the centre, or blocks of cl
st and h st.

LEAF WITH TWO SCROLLS, 60/2 LINEN

Techniques used in the motif – cl st, h st, d st edge, four-about-
the-pin edge, a scroll, raised edge sewings, braid no.3, hanging
in a pair of bobbins and b st.

Photo 34   Leaf with two scrolls

Fig. 58   Leaf with two scrolls

Method of working the motif

1. Prepare the pricking as previously explained.
2. At *a* hang on four pairs of bobbins. Start to work the scroll
increasing to five pairs as soon as possible.
3. Using cl st finish working the short braid, using a d st edge at
each side.

4. At *b* start to work the four-about-the-pin edge. Work the first side in cl st. Hang in two pairs of bobbins as the braid widens – seven pairs of bobbins in total.

5. When *c* is reached, use this pin to pivot and b st round the top of the leaf in cl st. With the threads used to make the b st, make a sewing through three of the lower loops about the pin. Leave this pair as a passive pair.

6. Work the h st side of the leaf, sewing into the four-about-the-pin edge. Take the crochet hook under both of the bars to make the sewing. Throw out two pairs of bobbins as the leaf narrows.

7. Make a sewing into *b*. Work the short length of braid in cl st and finish the motif by working the scroll. Cut off the threads close to the lace.

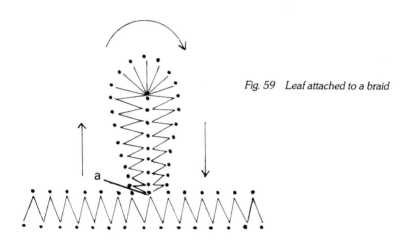

Fig. 59   *Leaf attached to a braid*

LEAF ATTACHED TO A BRAID, 60/2 LINEN

You will find this leaf in many of the traditional patterns. It is worked in a similar way to the *Leaf with two scrolls*, using seven pairs of bobbins. The pairs used to work the leaf are sewn into the pinloops and the edge of the braid. Care must be taken not to put any strain on the edge of the braid when firming the passive threads.

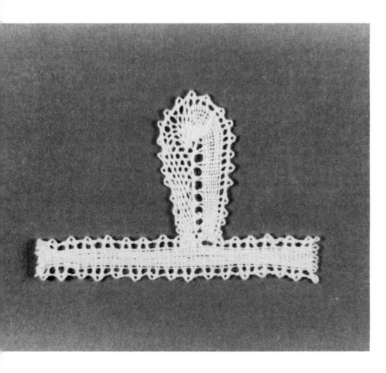

Photo 35   Leaf attached to a braid

When the five pairs have been sewn into the edge of the braid at *a*, it will be necessary to support these threads by putting the tip of the pin close to the braid so as to hold the sewings securely. The change from cl st to h st is made at the top centre pin. Take great care not to pull the passive threads when turning the top of the leaf. When the leaf has been worked, sew out the five pairs of bobbins into the braid, one pair at a time.

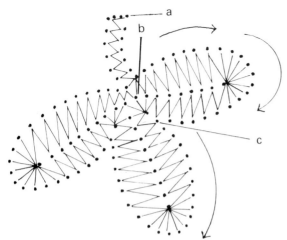

Fig. 60   *Drieblad leaf (shown on following page)*

DRIEBLAD – THREE-BLADED LEAF, 60/2 LINEN

Photo 36   Drieblad, three-bladed leaf

This leaf is worked using several techniques, and care should be taken to note where the b st are worked at the base of the three leaves.

Techniques used in the motif – cl st, h st, braid no.3, d st edge, four-about-the-pin edge, raised edge sewings, hanging in a pair of bobbins, throwing out a pair of bobbins and b st.

Method of working the motif

1.   At *a* put up four pins. Hang on five pairs of bobbins, two pairs on the fourth pin. Following the direction of the worker line, work the short braid.

2.   B st are worked round the base of the leaf in cl st. At *b* change to four-about-the-pin edge, keeping the outside edge worked as before in d st. Work this side of the blade, adding three more pairs of bobbins as the blade widens.

3.   Turn the top part of the blade as in *Leaf attached to a braid*, using cl st until the top part of the leaf has been worked. Remove the pin. Take the pair used for the b st and sew one of the threads through the three lower loops about the pin. Slide the other thread through the loop. Firm the threads.

4. Work the second side of the leaf in h st, making the sewing under both bars about the pin. As the blade narrows throw out one pair.

5. Work the b st at the base of the braid, and the sewings at *b* and *c*. Hang in a pair of bobbins and work the four-about-the-pin edge.

6. Work all the blades in this manner. Finish with five pairs of bobbins.

7. Sew the pairs into the centre pinloop. Tie and cut off the threads close to the lace.

A PAIR OF LEAVES WITH A VEIN, 60/2 LINEN

This leaf is worked with the same techniques as is used in the Drieblad leaf. The inner edge is raised and a d st edge is worked around the outer edge of the leaf. The top of the leaf is turned with b st and the stitch is changed at the centre pin from cl st to h st.

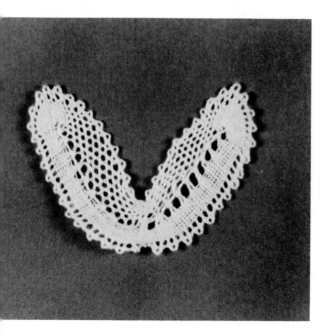

Photo 37   Pair of leaves with a vein

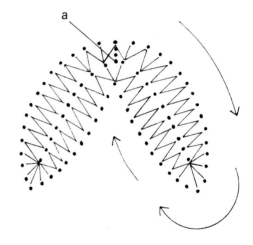

Fig. 61   A pair of leaves with a vein

Techniques used in the motif – cl st, h st, four-about-the-pin edge, raised edge sewings, d st edge and b st.

Method of working the motif

1. At *a* put up four pins and hang on seven pairs of bobbins. Work the leaf as directed for the Drieblad leaf, back stitching on

the centre pin. Arrows show the direction for working this leaf. Change from cl st to h st at the centre pin at the tip of the leaf.

2. Between the two leaves you will need to b st on the centre pin, before starting to work the second leaf, first in h st and the last side in cl st.

3. When the second leaf has been worked, sew the threads into the starter pinloops, one pair into one loop. Tie the threads off in the usual way. Cut off the threads close to the lace.

A PAIR OF LEAVES, STARTING AND FINISHING AT THE TIP OF THE LEAF, 60/2 LINEN

Techniques used in the motif – cl st, d st edge, braid no.3, twists and a single leaf.

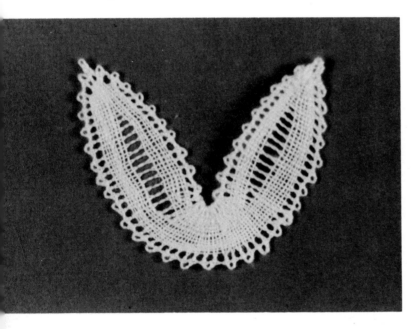

Photo 38   Pair of leaves, starting and finishing at the tips

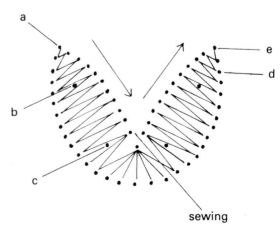

Fig. 62   A pair of leaves, starting and finishing at the tip of a leaf

Method of working the motif

1. Follow the instructions, for working a single leaf, setting up the leaf at *a*. The workers are used to make the vein in the centre between *b* and *c*. Make one twist with the workers on the first row, and two twists on the other rows, this being known as a 'ladder'.
2. At the base of the leaf, b st are used to pivot and turn the threads into the second leaf. Remember to make a sewing through the three lower loops around the pin.
3. The second leaf has a 'ladder' vein.
4. When *d* is reached four pairs are thrown out, two at each edge of the next four rows.
5. Two pairs are left to work the centre pin. Work the d st, take the pairs to the back of the pin.
6. Using one of the pairs already thrown out, open them, and place the two pairs between the threads. Tie the threads, holding the last two pairs close to the lace. Tie them three times and cut off the threads.

A SCROLL

The scroll and braid acts as a framework for Bruges Flower lace. They outline and intertwine among flowers and leaves. They are linked to these features of the design by filling stitches.
Techniques used in the motif – cl st, b st, d st edge, hanging in a pair, throwing out a pair and a sewing.

Setting up a scroll

1. Put up a pin at *a* and hang on four pairs of bobbins. The first pair on the left will not be used. The second pair will be the worker pair. The third pair must be twisted three times and the fourth pair twisted once.
2. Take the workers through the third pair and then work the edge stitch with the fourth pair at *b*.
3. Work back to the left through the passive pair in cl st.
4. Twist the workers twice. Lead the workers behind the pin at *a* and back under the passive pair that was left hanging.
5. The scroll will increase in width as it is worked. Pairs must now be added to accommodate the width of the scroll. Look at the diagram and you will notice where the pairs are hung in. The number of pairs added to the scroll will depend upon the thickness of the thread and the width of the scroll.

Photo 39   A scroll

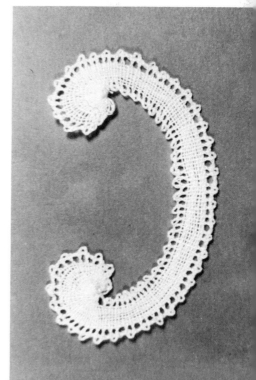

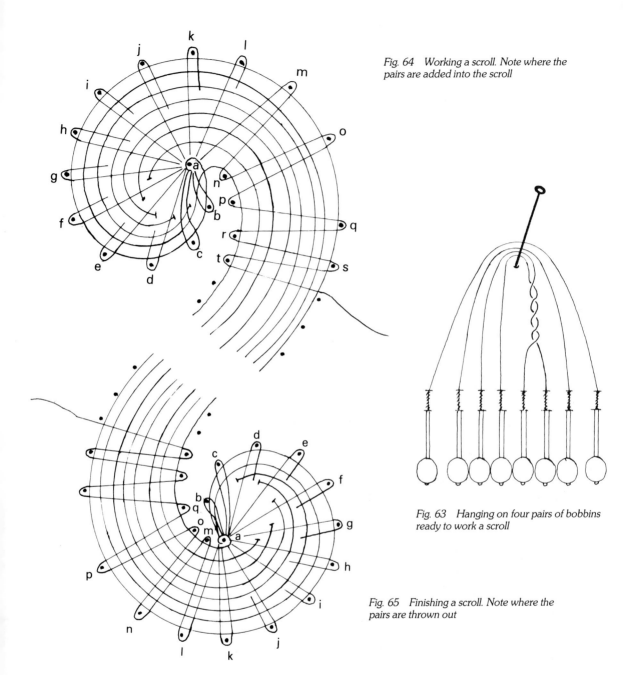

Fig. 64 Working a scroll. Note where the pairs are added into the scroll

Fig. 63 Hanging on four pairs of bobbins ready to work a scroll

Fig. 65 Finishing a scroll. Note where the pairs are thrown out

6. The scroll is worked in this way until pin *m* is reached, when one can work horizontally. Remove the pin at *a* and using a crochet hook draw a loop through three of the underlying threads about the pin. Place the other thread through the loop and firm both threads. This pair is now used in the normal way to work the edge stitch. Continue to work the braid.

Finishing a scroll

1. Complete the working at pin *b*, and work back to pin *a*, having thrown out the same number of threads as were hung in.

2. Take out the pin at *a*, and using the first passive pair used to make the b st, sew into the underlying three loops about the pin at *a*. The three remaining pairs should be passed through this loop.

3. Tie the loop pair firmly, and tighten all the other pairs so that the scroll is even. Open a pair which has been thrown out, lay the four pairs between these threads. Tie the four pairs down to the scroll with this pair.

4. Some of these pairs may be used to work the filling. Those not needed may be cut off close to the lace.

COCKTAILS – A SUPPER SERVIETTE, TANNE THREAD NO.30

Techniques used in the motif – braid no.2 and leaf with two scrolls.

Photo 40   Cocktails, a supper serviette

Fig. 66   Pricking for the Cocktails *serviette*

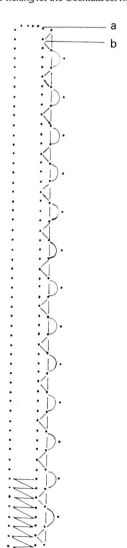

Method of working the motif

1. Start by working the braid, using seven pairs of bobbins. Several b st are worked at the corner. Allow an extra two centimetres in length. This will allow the lace to be eased on to the edge.
2. Work the leaf with two scrolls.
3. Using a matching thread over-cast the braid on to the small serviette, easing in the fullness. Press flat.
4. Catch-stitch the leaf in place in the corner.

MARIGOLD, 60/2 LINEN

Techniques used in the motif – flower no. 1, filling no. 1, a tally, braid no. 3, starting and finishing a scroll, sewings, plait-with-picot and edging no. 3.

Photo 41   Marigold

Method of working the motif

1. Work flower no. 1 and filling at *a*.
2. Work the two long scrolls *b*, using seven pairs of bobbins. Sewings are worked at *c* and *d*.
3. Work the plait-with-picot areas at *e*.
4. Work the two small scrolls *f*, five pairs of bobbins are needed.
5. Work the filling and the tally *g*.

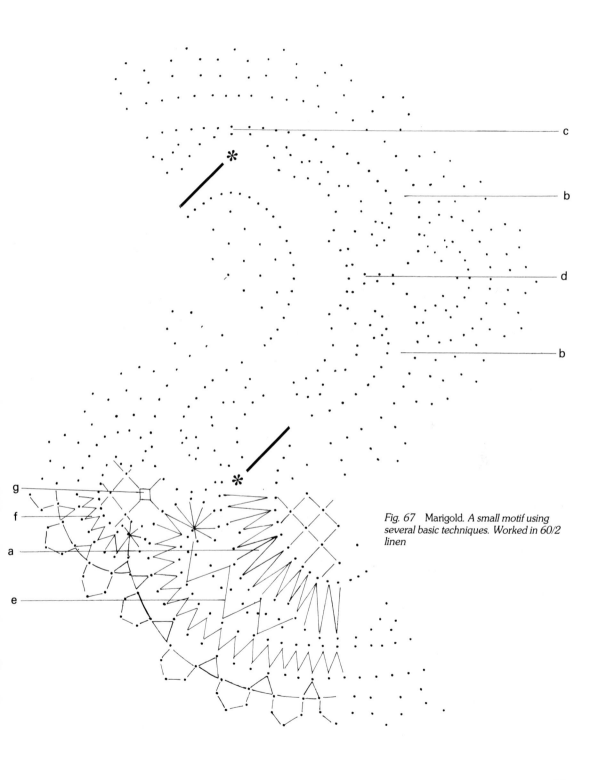

Fig. 67 Marigold. *A small motif using several basic techniques. Worked in 60/2 linen*

VALENTINE'S DAY, 60/2 LINEN

Techniques used in the motif – starting and finishing a scroll, braid no.3, filling no.3 and edging no.1

Photo 42   Valentine's Day

Method of working the motif

1. Work the scrolls; starting at *a* and finishing at *b*, using seven pairs of bobbins. Note the sewings at *c*.
2. Work the filling, and avoid any unnecessary cut-offs.
3. Work the edging starting at *d*.

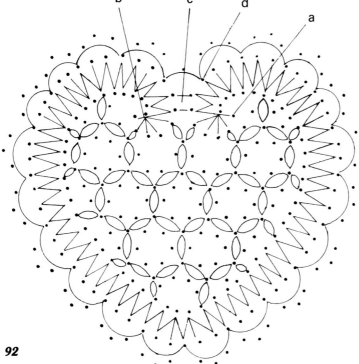

Fig. 68   Valentine's Day

LILLIAN, TANNE THREAD NO.30

Techniques used in the motif – leaf with a raised vein, sewings, hanging in pairs, throwing out pairs, b st, four-about-the-pin edge, raised edge sewings, cl st, h st, braid no.1 and d st edge.

Method of working the motif

1. Study the photograph and the pattern. Work the lily first. Set up the motif at *a*, using six pairs of bobbins. Each petal has a raised vein, and a d st edge. Hang in one more pair as the leaf widens. Follow the worker line.

2. Change to h st when the top pin has been worked, and change to cl st halfway through the b st at the base of each leaf.

3. Work the stem. Sew five pairs into the lily and work the stem

Photo 43 Lillian

using braid no.1. Tie off. These threads may be sewn through to the WS of the fabric.

4. At *c* start to work the leaf sewing in four pairs and increasing to six pairs. Use a d st edge and three twists about the pin on the

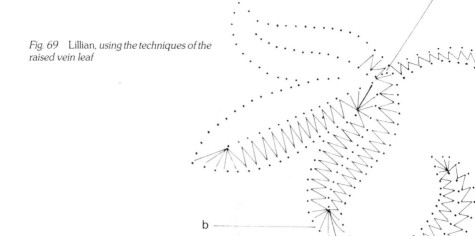

Fig. 69 Lillian, *using the techniques of the raised vein leaf*

inner edge. Sew into these pinloops when working the second side.

5. At *d* start to work the second leaf sewing in four pairs and increasing to six pairs.

6. Work the first side in cl st, and the second side in h st, sewing to the stem as and when necessary.

BLOSSOM TIME, 80/2 LINEN

Techniques used in the motif – flower no.10, d st edge braid, b st, crossing of two braids, filling no.4, a false plait, sewings, a tally and edging no.3.

Photo 44 Blossom Time

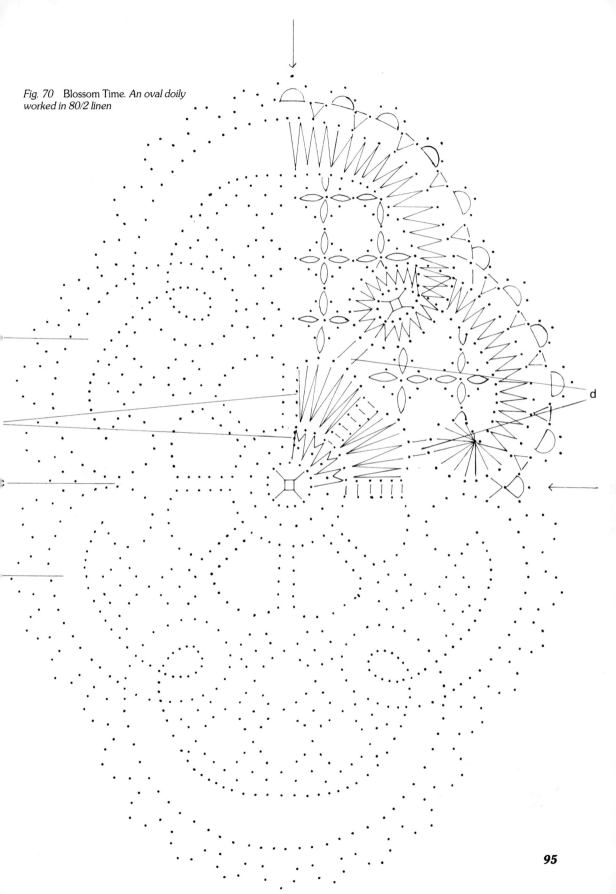

Fig. 70 Blossom Time. *An oval doily worked in 80/2 linen*

d

Method of working the motif

1. Work flower no. 10 a.
2. Work the scrolls and braids b, using ten pairs of bobbins. Sewings are made at c, and false plaits at d.
3. Work the filling. Work out the route to avoid any cut-offs.
4. Work the edging.

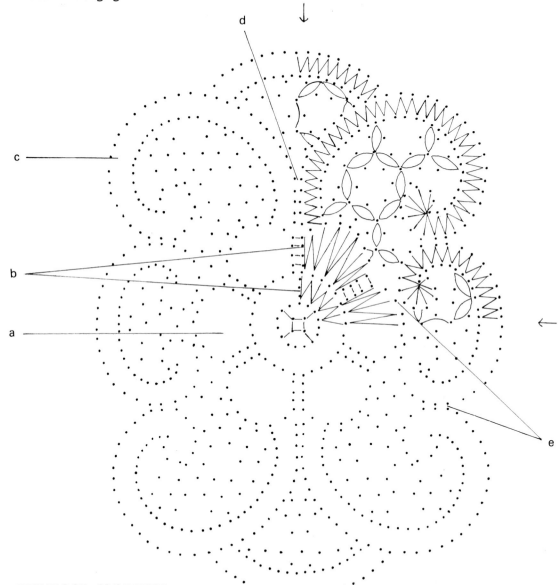

PRIMROSE, 60/2 LINEN

Techniques used in the motif – flower no. 7, braid no. 3, starting and finishing a scroll, filling no. 3, sewings (*page 32*) and a tally.

Fig. 71 Primrose. Doily worked in 60/2

Method of working the motif

Photo 45 Primrose

1. Work flower no. 7 *a*. Set up in a continuous line *b*. Note the sewings at *d* and *e*.
2. Work the scrolls and braids, using seven pairs of bobbins.
3. Work the two short braids, using seven pairs also.
4. Work the filling.

THE CHINESE ROSE, 60/2 LINEN

Techniques used in the motif – flower no.9, plaits, d st, plaits-with-picots, sewing in a pair, sewing out a pair and a single leaf.

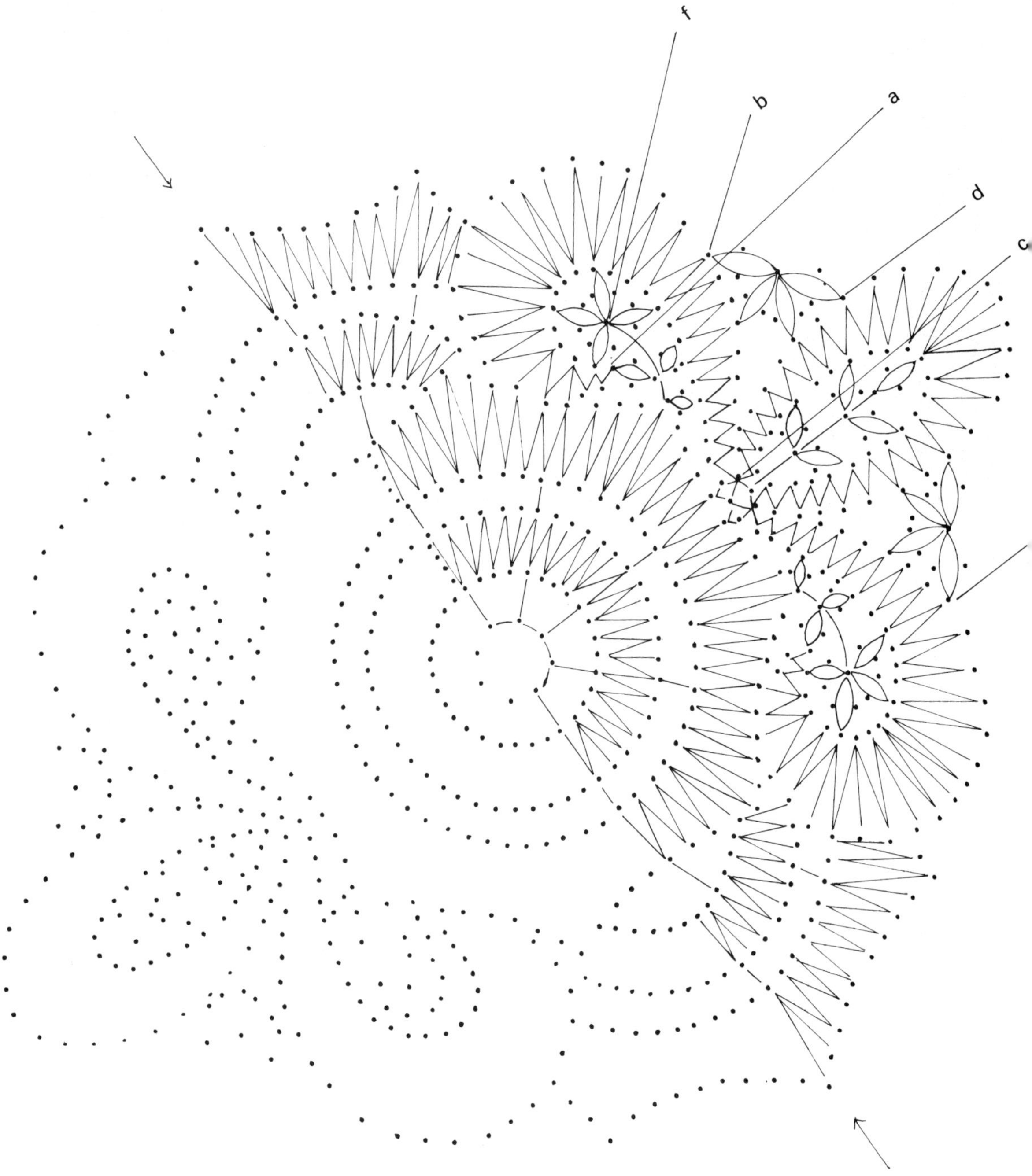

Fig. 72 The Chinese Rose

Method of working the motif

1. Work flower no.9.
2. Set up the leaves at a and hang in two extra pairs. Throw out one pair at b, five pairs remain at c.
3. Work the plait-with-picots from d and e.
4. Work the fillings inside the leaves.
5. Work the two quarter flowers.

Photo 46a The Chinese Rose, *designed and worked by Zus Boelaars*

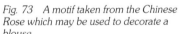

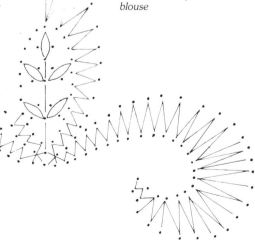

Fig. 73 A motif taken from the Chinese Rose which may be used to decorate a blouse

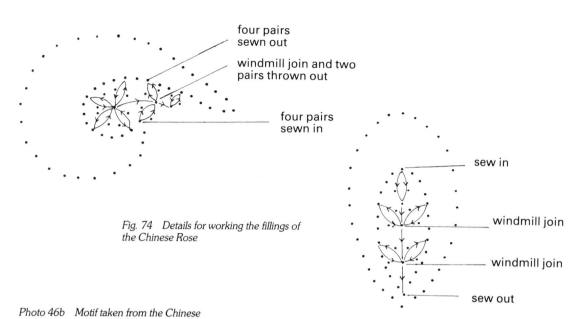

four pairs
sewn out

windmill join and two
pairs thrown out

four pairs
sewn in

*Fig. 74   Details for working the fillings of
the Chinese Rose*

sew in

windmill join

windmill join

sew out

*Photo 46b   Motif taken from the Chinese
Rose*

8

Further projects

You should, at this stage, have practised the basic techniques of the lace, and developed a good knowledge of Bruges Flower lace. In this chapter I have designed several advanced pieces which have practical applications. They differ in size and appearance from those offered earlier. Keep in mind the basic principles of lacemaking. Wind the bobbins correctly, use the suggested threads, and firm them frequently in order to attain the correct tension. Allow a short length of thread only between pin and bobbin. Keep the pillow covered when not in use.

ANNABELLE – A TRAY CLOTH CORNER, 60/2 LINEN

Techniques used in the motif – starting and finishing a scroll, braid no.3, a single leaf, a pair of leaves, a leaf attached to a

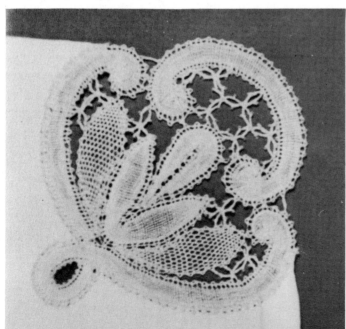

Photo 47 Annabelle, a tray cloth, worked by Mary Moseley and designed by the author

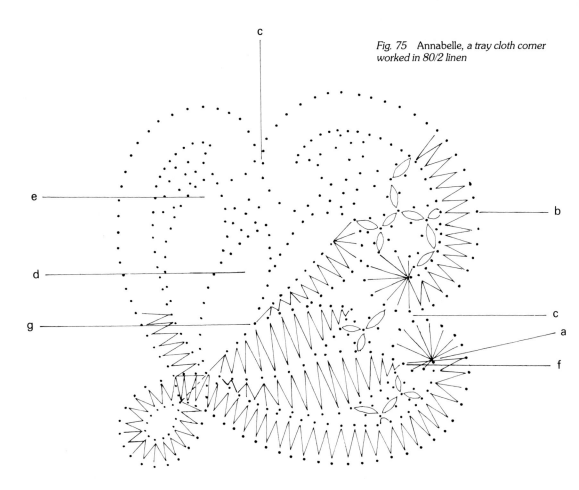

Fig. 75 Annabelle, *a tray cloth corner worked in 80/2 linen*

braid, crossing of two braids, filling no.3, sewings and a false plait.

Method of working the motif

1. Start to work the motif by working the scroll and braid *a*, using ten pairs of bobbins, and finishing with a second scroll.
2. The small upper scroll and braid *b* is worked next, using the same number of bobbins. Sewings and a false plait are made at *c*.
3. Work the pair of leaves at *d*, using cl st.
4. The lower leaves at *e* are worked next, in h st. Set up the leaf by sewing the two pairs into the pinloop of the scroll at *f*, and continue as directed. Sewings are made into the braid and the pinloops of the leaves.
5. Work the leaf attached to a braid (centre), sewing in four pairs at *g*.
6. Finally work the filling.

SARAJANE – A FINGER PLATE OR A WINE TRAY DECORATION, 60/2 LINEN

Techniques used in the motif – flower no.4, a scroll, dividing a braid and a single leaf, h st vein.

Fig. 76 Sarajane, a finger plate or tray motif, worked in no.30 Tanne thread

Photo 48 Sarajane, *a finger plate or a wine tray decoration*

Method of working the motif

1. Work flower no. 4
2. Work the four leaves with a h st vein.
3. Work the R and LH scrolls and braids increasing to seven pairs of bobbins in all. Start with the scroll and sew out into the flower.
4. At *a* start to work the centre braid, increasing to seven pairs. Sewings are made at each side of the braid *b*.
5. Divide this braid for the two small braids *c*.
6. Work the braids at the other side.

Fig. 77 Emma, *a place mat worked in 60/2 linen*

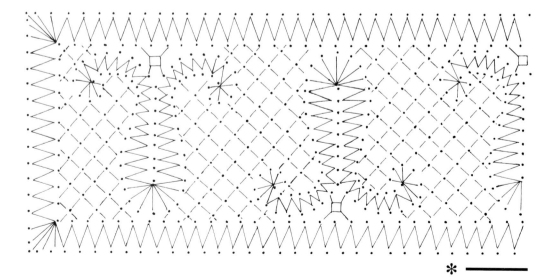

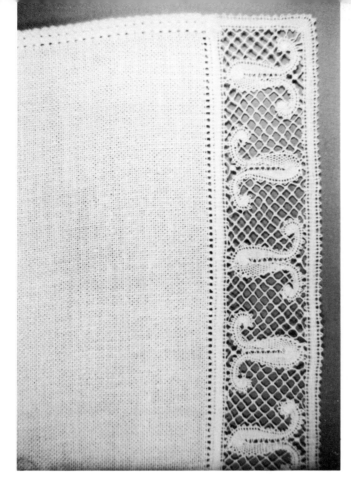

Photo 49   Emma, *a place mat*

EMMA – A PLACE MAT, 60/2 LINEN

Techniques used in the motif – a leaf with two scrolls, braid no. 3,
a tally, filling no. 1, sewings and b st.

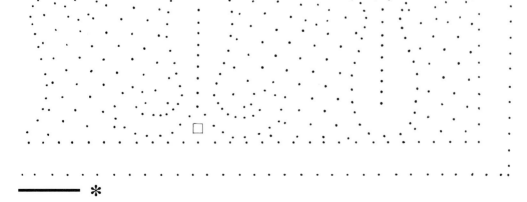

———— ✳

Method of working the motif

1. Work the centre leaf with two scrolls, and those at each side of it.
2. Using eight pairs of bobbins work the braid. B st are used at the corners, and sewings are made to attach the braid to the leaves.
3. Work all the tallies.
4. Finally work the filling, Dieppe ground, filling no. 1.

The motif is sewn to a piece of linen, using hem stitch. The other three edges are neatened with a four-sided stitch.

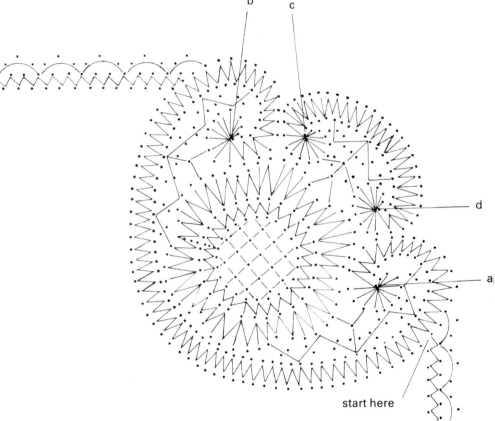

Fig. 78 Rebecca-Anne, a handkerchief corner and edging, worked in 120/2 linen

b

c

d

a

start here

REBECCA-ANNE – A HANDKERCHIEF, 120/2 LINEN

Techniques used in the motif – flower no.3, starting and finishing a scroll, braid no.3, plait-with-picot and edging no.1.

Method of working the motif

1. Work flower no.3, using six pairs of bobbins for the inner circle and ten pairs for the petals.

2. Next work the scroll and braid. Using eight pairs of bobbins start at *a* and finish at *b*.

3. Work the small scrolls and braid, using eight pairs of bobbins, starting at *c* and finishing at *d*. Note where the sewings are worked.

4. Work the plait-with-picot filling.

5. Set up the edging where indicated and work 3cm extra on each of the whole sides and 2cm on the partial sides. This allows the lace to be eased on to the edge of the handkerchief.

Photo 50   Rebecca-Anne, a handkerchief, worked by Christine Corner and designed by the author

STEPHANIE – A SPECTACLE CASE, 80/2 LINEN

Techniques used in the motif – flower no.3, a tally, a scroll, braid no.3, braid no.1, a Drieblad leaf, plait-with-picot, a false plait and sewings.

Method of working the motif

1. Start to work the braid. At *a*, put up a pin and hang on three pairs of bobbins. Follow the worker line and increase the number of bobbins to six pairs. Complete the braid to the base of the Drieblad leaf.

2. Hang in one more pair and work the leaf. Sew the five

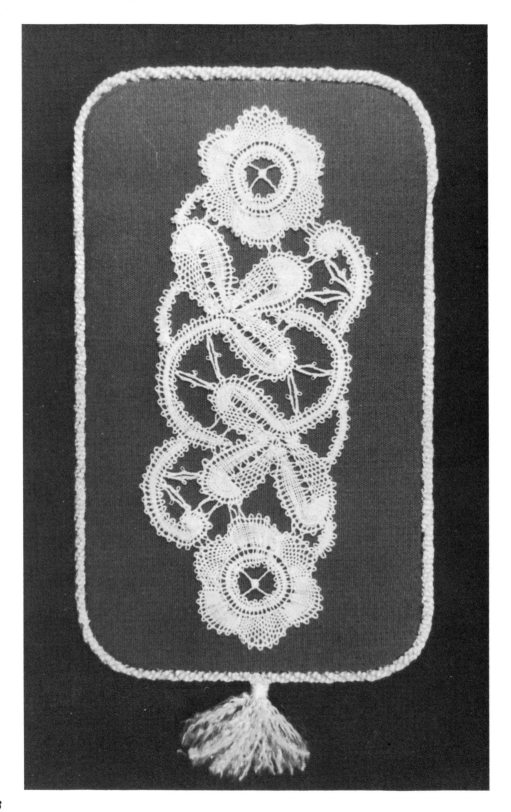

Photo 51   Stephanie, *a spectacle case*

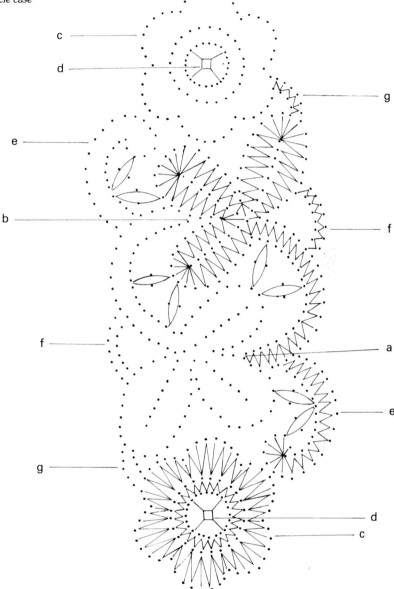

Fig. 79   Stephanie, *a spectacle case, worked in 80/2*

remaining pairs into the centre pinloop.

3. Work the second Drieblad leaf setting it up at *b*, and follow the worker line. Sewings, false plaits and the plait-with-picots are worked as the leaf progresses.

4. The flowers *c*, are worked next. Use five pairs for the inner circle and eight pairs for the petals. A tally, *d*, is worked in the centre. Note where the sewings are worked.

5. Work the braid and scroll at *e*, using six pairs of bobbins, remembering to work the plait-with-picots, and the sewings. The second set of plait-with-picots will not have a loop to sew into because the scroll has not yet been worked. Put up a pin between the pairs and work the second plait-with-picot.
6. Work the simple braids *f* and *g*, using four pairs of bobbins.

ROSEMARIE – A COLLAR, 60/2 LINEN

Techniques used in the motif – flower no. 2, braid no. 3, crossing of two braids, filling no. 1, plait-with-picot, a tally, leaf attached to a braid and sewings.

Method of working the motif

1. Start by working the flowers, using 12 pairs of bobbins, and setting them up at *a*.
2. Work filling no. 1 in the centre of each flower.
3. Work the braid. Put up four pins at *b* and hang on seven pairs

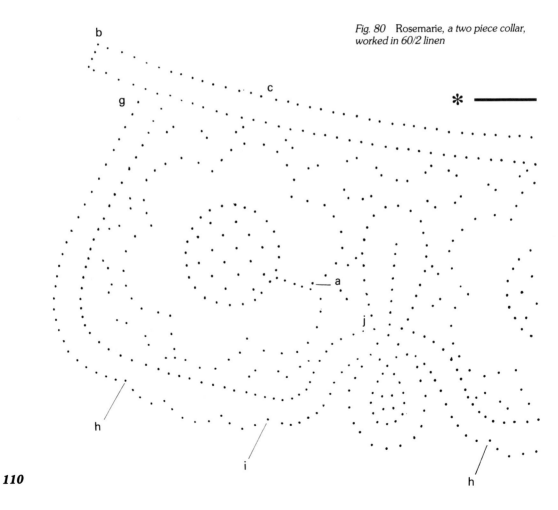

Fig. 80   Rosemarie, *a two piece collar, worked in 60/2 linen*

Photo 52a   Rosemarie, a collar, worked by Toos Driessens and designed by the author

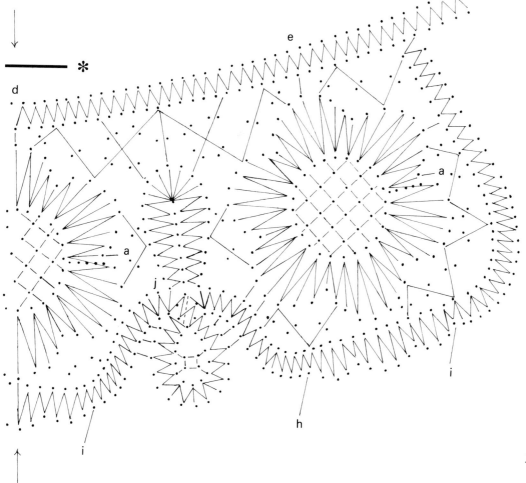

111

of bobbins. Note where the false plaits are worked at *c, d* and *e.*
Tie and cut off the threads at *f.*

4. Work the outer braid and at *g* sew in seven pairs of bobbins,
using the loops and edge of the braid to make the sewings.
Between *h* and *i,* h st is used. Note the false plaits, and the
crossing of the two braids.

5. The leaves are worked next. Sew in five pairs at *j.* Follow the
worker line carefully, and sew out the pairs into the braid.

6. Work the plait-with-picots to join all the features together.

7. Work a second collar in the same way.

WILD ROSE – AN APRON, 60/2 LINEN

Techniques used in the motif – flower no.8, a scroll, braid no.3,
filling no.1, a single leaf, cl st and h st sections, a false plait and
edging no.3.

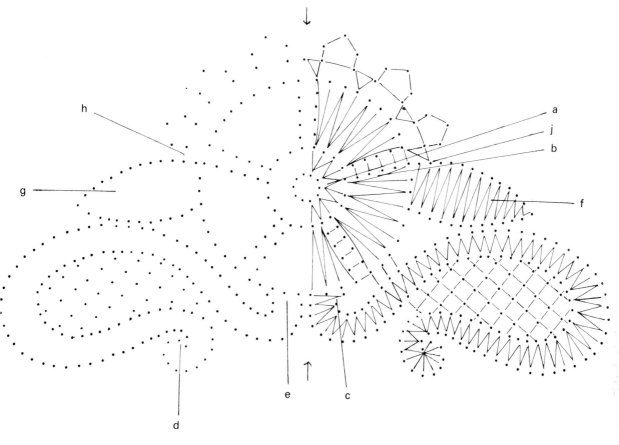

Fig. 81 Wild Rose, *a motif for an apron,*
worked in 60/2 linen

Photo 53a Wild Rose, *the large motif*
used on the apron

Method of working the motif

1. Work flower no.8, setting up the inner circle at *a* and the petals at *b*.
2. The scroll and braid *c* are worked next, requiring eight pairs of bobbins. Note where the three false plaits are worked. The second braid and scroll *d*, are worked next, setting up at *e*, and finishing with a scroll.
3. Complete the filling, using filling no.1.
4. Now work the two single leaves, *f* and *g*, using cl st and h st sections. Sewings are used to join the braids and leaves. Pairs are sewn out at *j*, one pair at a time.

The small motif

1. Work flower no.8 as before.
2. Sew in four pairs of bobbins at *a*, and work edging no.3. Sew out the pairs at *b*, one pair at a time.

The motifs are sewn to the apron using a fine thread, catch-stitch and hemming.

Photo 53b Wild Rose, *the small motif used on the pocket of the apron*

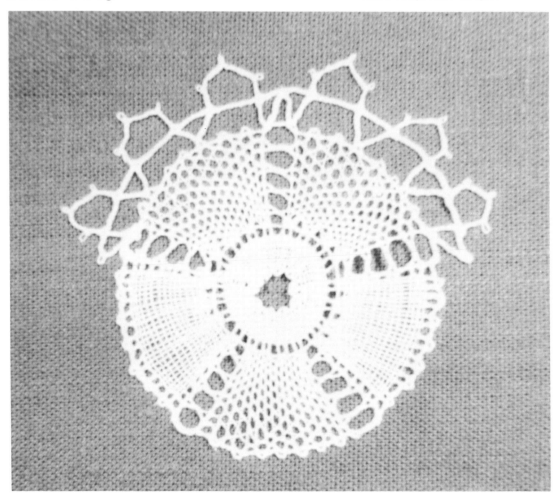

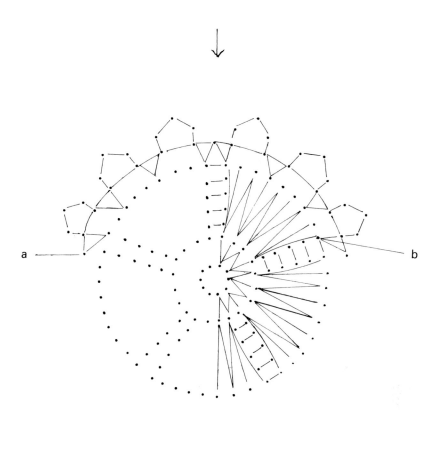

a

b

Fig. 82 Wild Rose, a small motif for the
pocket of an apron, worked in 60/2 linen

Bibliography

Channer, C.C., *Lacemaking Point Ground*, Dryad Press Ltd

d'Arcy, Eithne, *Irish Crochet Lace*, Dryad Press Ltd

Dye, Gilian, *Beginning Bobbin Lace*, Dryad Press Ltd

Fisher, Jennifer, *Torchon Lace for Today*, Dryad Press Ltd

Hardeman, Henk, *Torchon Patterns*, Dryad Press Ltd

Jones, Rebecca, *Complete Book of Tatting*, Dryad Press Ltd

Konior, Mary, *A Pattern Book of Tatting*, Dryad Press Ltd

Lovesey, Nenia, and Barley, Catherine, *Venetian Gros Point Lace*, Dryad Press Ltd

O'Cleirigh, Nellie, *Carrickmacross Lace*, Dryad Press Ltd

O'Conner, Christine, *Irish Lace Making*, Dryad Press Ltd

Stillwell, Alexandra, *Drafting Patterns for Torchon Lace*, Dryad Press Ltd

Withers, Jean, *Mounting and Using Lace*, Dryad Press Ltd

York, Sheila, *Projects in Tatting*, Dryad Press Ltd

Suppliers

UK

Alby Lace Centre
Cromer Road
Alby
Norwich
Norfolk

Frank Herring and Sons
27 High West Street
Dorchester
DT1 1UP

Honiton Lace Shop
44 High Street
Honiton
Devon

D.J. Hornsby
149 High Street
Burton Latimer
Kettering
Northants

Capt. J.R. Howell
19 Summerwood Lane
Halsall
Nr Ormskirk
Lancs L39 8RG

Sebalace
76 Main Street
Addingham
Ilkley
West Yorks
LS29 0PL

A. Sells
49 Pedley Lane
Clifton
Shefford
Beds

C. & D. Springett
251 Hillmorton Road
Rugby
Warwicks
CV22 5BE

Enid Taylor
Valley House Craft Studio
Ruston
Scarborough
N. Yorks YO13 9QE

George White
Delaheys Cottage
Thistle Hill
Knaresborough
North Yorks

European

Cibeles B V
Vijverlaan 497
2925 VH Krimpen aan den
Ijssel
The Netherlands

Scharlacken
Philipstockstraat 5 & 7
B 8000 Brugge
Belgium

't handwerkhuisje
Katelijnestraat 23
8000 Brugge
Belgium

't Vlaskeldertje
St Annastraat 189
6525 GM
Nijmegen
The Netherlands

Index